MANAGEMENT CONTROL AND INFORMATION

MANAGEMENT CONTROL AND INFORMATION

Studies in the Use of Control Information by Middle Management in Manufacturing Companies

R. BERESFORD DEW
Professor of Management Sciences

and

KENNETH P. GEE
Lecturer in Management Sciences
University of Manchester Institute
of Science and Technology

A HALSTED PRESS BOOK

John Wiley & Sons
New York – Toronto

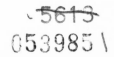

First published in the United Kingdom 1973 by
The Macmillan Press Ltd

Published in the U.S.A. and
Canada by Halsted Press, a
Division of John Wiley & Sons, Inc.,
New York

Library of Congress Cataloging in Publication Data

Dew, R   Beresford.
    Management control and information.

    "A Halsted Press book."
    Bibliography: p.
    1. Budget in business. 2. Management information
systems. 3. Middle managers. I. Gee, Kenneth P.,
joint author. II. Title.
HF5550.D39   658.4'03   73–3033
ISBN 0–470–21170–9

Printed in Great Britain

Contents

Preface

As an organisation grows, so there will develop, for its more effective management, an increasing dependence on formal information systems.

For some years, longer ago than I care to remember, I managed a large factory. In my experience, the information provided for my use by the formal control system was generally irrelevant to my problems. I also learnt that my experience was in no way unique. Over a long period therefore, and more recently with Dr Kenneth Gee, I have been interested in exploring this anomaly.

What is the explanation of the fact that managers at middle levels in industry either do not, or cannot, use the information by which they are expected to exercise control? A very low utilisation is frequently found by research, but research studies are often filed away to gather dust. Managers have neither time nor inclination to pore over academic theses. The authors of this book therefore summarise, in plain English, a number of studies in management control information, and trust that the form of a short and simple exposition will be acceptable. They hope that a better understanding of the value and impact of information systems (to which higher levels of executive management are often expected to turn before reaching their decisions) may thus be achieved.

The findings of these studies seem to point to several lessons as to when management control systems may be most effective.

Part I, as an introduction to research in management information, describes the results of studies in the narrow field of budgetary control. The implications of these, both for executives in manufacturing organisations and for management accountants, will be allowed largely to speak for themselves and are sufficiently revealing.

Part II is concerned with studies in management information

as such. These studies are described in rather more detail, being concerned with a range of critical features. This more detailed approach is also intended to attract management to the challenges of research studies, with a view to an improvement in management information systems as commonly conceived.

Part III is concerned with some of the lessons, and contains a number of circumstantial deductions and ideas concerning the management process in industry. These lessons are presented in the form of twelve reflections on the circumstances in which management control information systems are likely to fulfil their purpose, or are likely to fail. The reflections in turn lead to a number of prescriptive summary conclusions.

November 1972   R. B. D.

An Introduction to the Problem

Systems of budgetary control are commonly provided for management by accountants. The accountants hope that the executive managers will thus manage their enterprises more effectively. But do the managers make use of the information that the accountants provide?

In one of the first studies of this question,[1] interviews in depth were undertaken with line managers and accountants in four factories. (These were of medium size, ranging between 200 and 1100 employees.) All had well-established budgetary control systems.[2]

In all, 60 middle managers were interviewed. It was found that 32 managers ignored their budgets entirely. Of the remaining 28 managers, 12 made only limited use of their budgets. They might, for example, refer to that part which related to output but not to that part which related to cost.

Thus only 16 of the 60 managers interviewed in these factories used the whole of their budgets. The four factories had different types of budgetary control system; but there was no significant

[1] A. M. A. Rahim, unpublished Ph.D. thesis (University of Manchester, 1966), researches with Professor R. Beresford Dew on 'Industrial Managers' Acceptance and Use of Budgetary Control Techniques: An Empirical Approach'. For brevity, this study will be referred to hereafter as the R study.

[2] The factories all belonged to the same group of companies in the paper industry. However, it was a highly decentralised, multi-product group in which factories were located throughout the United Kingdom, and each factory was almost autonomous. Two of the factories were engaged in the production of corrugated cases, one was engaged in multi-process printing and the fourth in carton packaging. These different products involved different technologies, and a variety of production processes.

difference between the factories in the proportions of the managers who used their budgets.

It seemed that the well-intentioned efforts of the accountants who operated the budgetary systems were largely wasted so far as the managers were concerned. The managers appeared to pay little attention to their predetermined standards of performance, or to the examination of achievement as depicted in the control returns. Whether or not the top management thought that achievement should be measured by reference to such control information, the middle managers in these companies evidently did not do so.

Additional studies were therefore undertaken in other, entirely distinct factories. Four more factories were selected, but from companies engaged in entirely different industries, and in no other way connected.[1] Further, departments in these factories were chosen for study by agreement with the management, as being departments whose managers were most likely to refer to their budgetary information.

25 managers were studied. Of these 25, 6 did not refer to their budgetary information. 13 made only some limited reference to it.

So, even in departments which were thought to be budget-conscious, in practice out of 25 managers no fewer than 19 made little or no use of the information provided.

No evidence was found in any company to support any hypotheses that failures to set up scientific standards or failures to implement reasonable systems of planning and control had caused the general lack of use of the budgets. Beneath a polite acceptance, there appeared in fact a general indifference in the executive management to the budgetary system provided to them for control purposes.

How is it possible that systems of budgetary control should in fact be so largely ignored by the managers for whose benefit they have been designed?

As a second question: is it possible that management control information as such, i.e. the wide range of formally presented information produced in many companies for purposes of

---

[1] i.e. mechanical engineering, electrical engineering, chemicals and food-processing. The companies were of quite different sizes, ranging from 300 to 20,000 operatives.

management, and not simply the accountants' information on outputs and costs, tends similarly, in practice, to be ignored by the managers – and if so, why?

These two questions evidently deserved examination.

The results of the research studies into the first question are to be found in Part I. Part II is concerned with the second question. Part III offers some reflections on the implications of the findings from these studies for all who are concerned with the production or use of control information by middle management in industry.

Part I

The first part of this book is concerned with budgetary control. Its foundations are examined in terms of six propositions. Each is reviewed in the light of research findings from studies in a number of companies with well-developed budgetary control systems.

We arrived at the somewhat arresting conclusion that, generally speaking, not a single one of the six conditions which may be thought necessary for successful budgetary control could be found in practice.

It is understandable that the budgetary control system should largely be ignored by the managers, when the conditions for its use are noticeable only by their absence. These conditions are:

1. That management responsibility must be clear.
2. That managers must see their standards and budgets as attainable.
3. That the budgetary control information must be understood by those for whom it is designed.
4. That training in budgetary control must be effective.
5. That the organisation of information production must be appropriate.
6. That managers must understand the purposes of the budgetary system.

I Six Propositions for Effective Budgetary Control

THE PROPOSITIONS OUTLINED

There are a great many ways of examining a company's budgetary control system. The central interest, in this case, was the apparent indifference of the executives at the middle levels of management, to whom information is provided for control purposes by management accountants.

A budgetary system can only provide an effective instrument if it meets certain requirements and conditions. Although particular conditions will no doubt apply in each case, it is likely that there are certain general considerations which must apply in all cases.

A number of the more commonly held assumptions were therefore selected, with a view to checking realities in a few industrial enterprises where budgetary control systems were firmly entrenched. *Inter alia*, we sought reasons for management indifference.

If one is to judge the value of a system, it is necessary first of all to establish the criteria which will be applied in making the judgement.

It is obviously not enough that a system has the appearance of being effective or ineffective. Either it does or it does not comply with the minimum conditions which are required for its successful performance.

If such conditions do not obtain, then it will be difficult, if not impossible, to assess the merits of the system as such.

Every system must, to some extent, be tailor-made to meet particular circumstances. But common sense at once suggests a number of conditions which should obtain at all times, in whose absence budgetary control can hardly be expected to be very effective. Their existence in practice should not be too difficult to check.

Probably the single most important condition is that the figures which are presented to the management should tell the truth. Truth, however, is not a simple matter. Economic truths in particular are commonly the subject of violent disagreement. This particular group of researches therefore concentrated on other requirements.[1]

But although these particular researches in middle management information systems were not specifically concerned with the question of truth in presentation, in a more general sense all the findings suggest that the truth (in some companies at least) appears in very different colours to different levels of management and to the functional specialists respectively.

Six conditions for effective budgetary control proposed themselves, and were stated as follows:

1. In so far as the managers are expected to act on the information provided, managements' authority and responsibility must be clear.
2. As the system depends on predetermined standards and budgets, and the periodical measurement of performance for comparison with such standards, the managers must have accepted the standards as being reasonable and attainable.
3. Budgetary control information must be understood by the

---

[1] But truth deserves at least a passing comment.

There is some evidence that the truth at the present time is so alarming for many companies that there is a marked reluctance to face it. Moreover, the units in which the measurements of financial performance are made are themselves shrinking. It is as if one were attempting to take decisions by reference to an india-rubber yardstick which is itself contracting.

Whether the figures presented to management represent the truth, or include a minor or a gross distortion of the truth, is now an urgent question for many organisations.

For example, if profit forecasts are adjusted to include depreciation on a replacement cost basis, and to provide for adequate resources to meet the loss in value under inflation of working capital – gross, as this is not allowable for taxation – it will be found that all too often the profit forecasts are in fact loss forecasts. Many performance returns suffer from the same comforting distortion. The basis of calculation of measurements like the return on investment now presents a problem of great significance.

managers, and, hopefully, understood in the same way by the individuals who produced it.

4. As some training or education in the use and value of budgetary control systems is required, gained on formal courses or simply by experience, this training must have been successful for the purposes intended.

5. As the budgetary control information flow will be affected by the suitability or otherwise of the management accounting organisation, this organisation must be appropriate.

6. If managers should misunderstand the purposes of the budgetary system, they may take inappropriate action on the information which that system produces for them; so the purposes of the system must be clear to the managers.

Some studies were therefore undertaken to see whether these six suggested foundation stones would be found to underlie the budgetary control systems of different factories.

It should be stressed again that at this stage in our inquiries we were concerned simply with what may be described as the conventional system of budgetary control, largely designed by management accountants and to be found in a great variety of industrial firms.

We were not, at this stage, concerned with the altogether broader challenges of management information systems as such, i.e. with the range of management information, formally produced by a variety of functional staff, from different parts of the organisation. To this wider field we shall come in due course, in Part II.

PROPOSITION I. THAT MANAGEMENT RESPONSIBILITY MUST BE CLEAR

The clarity of managerial responsibility was examined in ten different companies within the steel industry.[1]

[1] I. M. E. Hilal, unpublished Ph.D. thesis (University of Manchester, 1966), researches with Professor R. Beresford Dew on 'The Factors Affecting Cost Control by Shop Floor Management in the British Iron and Steel Industry'. The companies studied were together responsible for just under 50 per cent of total United Kingdom steel output. They varied in size from

Two levels of management were selected: senior management below the level of the board, and the middle managers responsible to those senior managers.

It was the general practice in all these companies to define the responsibilities of senior management jobs formally, and in writing. The responsibilities of the middle management were sometimes so defined and were sometimes a matter of experience.[1]

The views of the senior managers as to their own areas of authority were compared with their job descriptions. The views of the middle management as to their areas of authority were compared with those of the senior management to whom they responded.

In both cases, the results were classified as either consistent or inconsistent. For a senior manager a consistent answer was one that tallied with his job description. An inconsistent answer was one which either omitted an important feature which was noted as being his responsibility on his job description, or alternatively included in his responsibility a feature which did not appear on his job description, and which was confirmed by the executive holding the job descriptions apparently to lie outside his jurisdiction.

The replies of the middle management were also classified as consistent or inconsistent, according to whether the views of the middle managers coincided with the views of the senior managers to whom they reported (see Table 1.1).

Of the 36 senior managers who were included in these studies, 30 defined their responsibility in accordance with official job descriptions. Six, however, gave answers which were inconsistent with their job descriptions.

But it was plain that, since the descriptions for these 6 senior managers had been prepared, operating conditions had changed. In these cases of inconsistency the job descriptions specified areas of jurisdiction which may have been more

---

3000 to 17,000 employees, and were located throughout England and Wales. For brevity, this study will be referred to hereafter as the H study.

[1] All the 36 senior managers interviewed had at some time drawn up formal job descriptions and agreed them with a member of top management (almost invariably the company secretary). Of the 406 middle managers interviewed, only 107 had agreed job descriptions.

appropriate to former conditions, but were regarded as inconsistent with present realities as seen by the senior managers.

The 406 middle managers included in these studies were confidently thought by the senior managers to know their jobs and the limits of their authority, and the nature of their responsibility. Yet no fewer than 186 of these managers gave definitions which were substantially at variance with the definitions of their authority provided by the senior managers.

Table 1.1

THE CONSISTENCY OF VIEWS EXPRESSED BY SENIOR AND MIDDLE MANAGERS AS TO THEIR AREAS OF JURISDICTION

Comparison between views of	*No. of answers which were* CONSISTENT	*No. of answers which were* INCONSISTENT	TOTAL
Senior managers and their job descriptions	30	6	36
Middle managers and senior managers	220	186	406

In nearly half the cases considered, the views of the senior managers as to the extent and the nature of the authority of their middle managers did not agree with the views of those middle managers. It appeared that the middle managers often saw their tasks in a different light. This was true even though the senior managers themselves may, in the past, have held these jobs at middle management levels.

There were sometimes differences, hitherto unrecognised, between the senior and middle management as to the nature of the middle management tasks. For example, of 226 middle managers with cost control responsibilities, only 132 defined these in a way which was consistent with the views of their superiors. The remaining 94 middle managers gave definitions which showed substantial differences of opinion between them and their superiors as to which costs were in fact under their control.[1,2]

---

[1] Conflicts of view concerning cost responsibilities were not confined to those between senior and middle line managers, e.g. middle managers and maintenance engineers often conflicted on the question of responsibility for maintenance cost in the production departments. Of 153 production

Formal job descriptions were evidently more reliable than general experience. Of the 30 middle managers who had agreed in writing with the higher management the costs which lay within their own control, only four produced inconsistent answers.

In only one of the companies studied was there a consistent practice of drawing up job descriptions for all middle as well as all senior managers. 21 of the 24 middle managers interviewed in this company stated that they found job descriptions of considerable value. Further, when a study was made of the attitudes of middle managers in other companies towards the formal definition of cost responsibilities, it was found that, of 382 managers, 237 were in favour while only 68 were opposed to this approach.[1]

If in practice senior and middle managers do not agree closely as to who is responsible for different middle management tasks and as to which among these tasks are the most important, they can hardly be expected to be in agreement about the nature of the information required for these tasks to be undertaken effectively.

But would the converse also be found to be true? Whether agreement about the responsibilities would carry with it agreement about the relative importance of various items of control information was a further question which evidently deserved to be studied later on (see Chapter 6).

It should be stressed that these findings, though they may appear to underline the advantages of job descriptions, are not necessarily to be regarded as powerful arguments in their favour. A job description may well be agreed between the managers. Nevertheless, its terms may be unnecessarily narrow: it may or may not give the middle management a comprehensive view of their tasks; it may or may not be encouraging.

(middle) managers, 134 thought that *they* were responsible, while of 26 maintenance engineers 23 thought that *they* were responsible.

[2] In the authors' subsequent studies, the most frequently encountered reason for not using an item of control information was that the manager receiving it considered it to cover a matter outside his control.

[1] Of the remaining 77 managers, 53 considered that formal definition of operating and cost responsibilities would have no effect on their actions, while 24 thought it would have some effect but were unable to say whether it would improve or worsen their management.

Moreover, there is some evidence that strict definitions, clear responsibilities and a formal structure may well be appropriate arrangements for organisations which are relatively stable, but that they make any form of innovation much more difficult. Organisations which are most ready to accept change may gain from having formal relationships and responsibilities not too closely defined. Such organisations may be highly successful, provided that their objectives are both clearly known and generally accepted.

But it is clear that when an organisation introduces a budgetary control system whose operation relies, *inter alia*, upon an assumption that the managers are clear among themselves about the extent and nature of executive responsibility for action, and it turns out that the managers are not so clear as was assumed to be the case, then that organisation is expecting too much of its control system. And in practice it appears that there may well be more substantial misunderstandings between the different levels of executive management as to the nature of the middle managements' problems and tasks than the managers themselves may have recognised.

But it is not sufficient that the line managers should be clear. It is equally necessary that those who prepare and produce the control information for the managers should themselves be clear.

406 middle managers in the H group of studies were asked whether, in their opinion, the actions of the foremen immediately subordinate to them had a significant effect on the cost of the final product (Table 1.2). 329 of these managers were convinced that this was the case,[1] while a further 47 thought that foremen had an influence but not a significant one. Eight senior management accountants in these ten companies were then asked why in fact they did not produce cost information for the foremen (Table 1.3). Some gave more than one reason. Seven were of the view that foremen had no influence on costs. Five thought the foremen would not appreciate such information. Three said they had no facilities for doing it, and two thought it would be unsafe.

Whether the accountants were right or wrong is not the

[1] 26 out of 36 senior managers interviewed also shared this view, as did 86 out of 129 of the foremen themselves.

point. There were evidently gulfs of misunderstanding between the managers and the accountants about the foremen's influence on results in terms of costs.

It is not only between the managers themselves but also between the managers and their accountants that the nature of management responsibility must be clear. The assumption that it is clear deserves to be subjected to test.

Table 1.2

WHETHER FOREMEN ARE IN A POSITION TO
HAVE A SIGNIFICANT INFLUENCE ON COST

Interviewee	A significant influence	A minor influence	No influence	Total interviewed
Departmental and assistant managers:				
Planning and progress and works records	80	21	14	115 .
Stores and spares, and raw materials	46	15	4	65
Production	170	9	12	191
Engineers (maintenance)	33	2	–	35
Total	329	47	30	406

Table 1.3

SENIOR ACCOUNTANTS' REASONS FOR NOT PROVIDING
FOREMEN WITH COST INFORMATION

Company ref. no.	Have no influence on cost	Not able to appreciate cost information	No facilities in cost office	Information would be unsafe
1	×	×		
2	×	×		
3	×			×
5	×			
6	×	×	×	
7	×		×	
8		×	×	
10	×	×		×
Total	7	5	3	2

PROPOSITION 2. THAT MANAGERS MUST CONSIDER THEIR STANDARDS AND BUDGETS TO BE ATTAINABLE

If managers participate in the establishment of their budgets, it may be assumed that they will therefore agree with them.[1]

In the course of the R group of studies, attention was turned to the extent to which middle managers had participated in the setting of their budgets and to the implications of this for their acceptance of those budgets.

There were three different situations:

1. Participation: the middle manager prepared his own budget and then submitted his budget for approval by higher management.
2. Consultation: the budgets were drawn up by higher management and agreed with the middle manager after consultation.
3. Non-consultation: either no consultation of any kind or only a nominal consultation, so that in effect the budgets remained as they had been originally.

The findings (see Table 1.4) showed, not unexpectedly, that managers who participated also used their budgetary control information to the greatest extent.

Next in order came the managers who were consulted. The managers who used their information least were those who did not enter into the budgetary process at all, central mandatory budgets being issued to them. These findings merely confirmed that participation improves middle managements' attitude towards control information and willingness to be involved in budgetary control functions.

But what is participation? In one of the companies studied, performance standards had been established quite recently with the application of method and work study techniques. During the installation there had been much consultation with all concerned, in particular with the managers themselves, before the standards were installed.

40 of the managers were asked, therefore, whether they considered that the standards set for their departments were

[1] See, for example, G. H. Hofstede, *The Game of Budget Control* (London: Tavistock Press, 1968) esp. p. 251.

attainable. Of these 40 managers, 12 said 'yes' and 28 said 'no'.

It was quite clear that although the managers had apparently approved the standards, or at least at the time had raised no particular objection to them, this was so far as they were concerned no more than a formal paper exercise. They never felt, in other words, at any time committed emotionally or managerially to the performance standards. They never, as the managers of those departments, had a real acceptance of the standards, or any determination to achieve them.

Table 1.4

RELATIONSHIP BETWEEN PARTICIPATION AND USE OF BUDGETARY INFORMATION

	No. of managers who PARTICIPATED *in budget setting*	*No. of managers* who WERE CONSULTED *about their budgets*	*No. of managers* who WERE NOT CONSULTED	TOTAL
No. of managers who made FULL USE of their budgets	10	1	1	12
No. of managers who made LIMITED USE of their budgets	20	8	7	35
No. of managers who DID NOT USE their budgets	4	6	28	38
Total	34	15	36	85

Note: With four degrees of freedom, the value of chi-square obtained from this table is 33·0, which is significant at the 5 per cent level.

This is a particularly difficult problem because no doubt it appeared at the time that the managers in fact were in agreement. They may even have stated formally that they agreed with the standards. They may well have done this because they did not fully appreciate the significance of the process; or they had a respect for cost and output information produced by sophisticated methods; or it may be that the standards appeared to be more or less the same as the standards that existed previously, and there appeared to be no difficulties at the time of the meeting.

But then the returns come in, with red figures on them, and questions are asked about the variances, and judgements are made in high places about the manager's performance. Even though he may not have objected at the time when they are set, the manager in his heart simply rejects those standards as being inappropriate, or unfair, or not relevant, should there be any change whatever in the circumstances.

What is the value of a standard, however carefully and formally established, for middle management performance if the middle managers in fact feel no personal commitment to that standard?

PROPOSITION 3. THAT BUDGETARY CONTROL INFORMATION MUST BE UNDERSTOOD

It may be assumed, either by those who prepare the information or by the higher management, that the middle managers understand the system which is given to them for control purposes. Such an inference may spring from the manager's educational background, or from his experience in his job, or from his participation in some specific training in the subject.

In the course of the R group of studies, these inferences were examined. Managers in eight different companies were divided into three educational groups:

1. Highly educated: managers with a degree or professional qualification.
2. Moderately educated: managers with a lesser qualification in further education, e.g. Higher National Diploma.
3. Poorly educated: managers without formal education beyond school level.

The managers were also grouped by reference to their budgets into those who made full use of their budgetary information, those who made only limited reference to it, and those who ignored their budgetary information entirely.

In the eight companies studied,[1] it was evident, as might be

---

[1] For details of these companies, see pp. xi–xii.

expected, that the better-educated managers made significantly more use of their budgets than did the managers who were less well educated (Table 1.5).[1]

Table 1.5
RELATIONSHIP BETWEEN GENERAL EDUCATION AND
USE OF BUDGETARY CONTROL INFORMATION

Use	Level of education		
	High	*Moderate*	*Poor*
Full	8	–	4
Limited	5	7	23
None	6	3	29

The influence of 'learning by doing', or job experience, was examined in two ways. First, managers with long experience of management without budgets – defined as managers who had worked without budgetary control information for more than ten years – were studied with reference to their use of budgetary control information. It was clear (Table 1.6) that such managers tended not to make use of their budgets when these were eventually provided.[2]

Table 1.6
RELATIONSHIP BETWEEN LONG EXPERIENCE
WITHOUT BUDGETS AND USE OF BUDGETARY
CONTROL INFORMATION

Use	Experience of managers	
	Long experience without budgets	*No long experience without budgets*
Full	3	9
Limited	23	12
None	32	6

[1] This is confirmed statistically by the application of a chi-square test, with four degrees of freedom. A value for chi-square of 19·0 is obtained, which is significant at the 5 per cent level.

[2] Again, statistical confirmation of this is provided by a chi-square test. With two degrees of freedom, the value of chi-square is 12·9, which is significant at the 5 per cent level. It was interesting that the three managers who had long experience without budgets but still made full use of budgetary information were all highly educated. This suggests that managers with a good educational background may be flexible enough to overcome the handicap of long experience without budgets.

Further confirmation of the above findings was obtained from a second approach, which consisted of examining those managers who had long experience with budgets. A slightly different definition was adopted here, for managers were considered to have had long experience with budgets if they had received budgetary information over a period of only three years. Studies of these managers gave rise to the results in Table 1.7. These are consistent with those of Table 1.6, for they show that managers having long experience with budgets tended to use these to a significantly greater extent than did managers without such experience.[1]

Table 1.7
RELATIONSHIP BETWEEN LONG EXPERIENCE
WITH BUDGETS AND USE OF BUDGETARY
CONTROL INFORMATION

| *Use* | *Experience of managers* | |
	Substantial experience with budgets	*Short experience with budgets*
Full	12	—
Limited	23	12
None	16	22

The effects of education and experience must therefore be kept in mind when attempting to discover by direct inquiry managements' understanding of the budgetary control information which the system provides.

152 production managers and assistant production managers were asked to say what they thought of their budgetary control information, with results as shown in Table 1.8.

That no fewer than 142 of the managers felt that there was not enough relevant information, while at the same time 40 thought there was too much detail, shows a great confusion; it seemed by no means clear to them how their reports should be interpreted. There seemed to be plenty of information but it did not seem entirely relevant. More than half the managers could not really see, from their information, where their responsibilities lay. No fewer than 150 out of 152 said that the information came too late for any effective action; this again may suggest a

[1] The value for chi-square in Table 1.7 is 12·5, which with two degrees of freedom is significant at the 5 per cent level.

Table 1.8

PRINCIPAL FEATURES AFFECTING THE USEFULNESS OF COST REPORTS AS A
COST CONTROL TOOL IN EIGHT COMPANIES

Interviewee	Too late for effective action	Basic information inaccurate	Money values do not suit requirements	Too many irrelevant details reported	Not enough relevant detail	Difficulty in identifying responsibilities	Total interviewed in eight companies
Production and assistant managers	150	47	143	40	142	106	152
Engineers (maintenance)	21	21	18	4	26	11	26
% to total	96	38	90	25	94	60	100

Note: Interviewees have identified more than one feature.

misunderstanding or a misinterpretation of the significance of the information.

The most startling of the answers refer to what is in effect a language barrier. Managers do not like the form in which their information is presented; it requires interpretation to mesh with their own thought-processes; it is not in the language of their discipline; they would prefer it to be expressed in a language which has meaning in that it is the medium in which they personally think and work, in terms of weights, or yards, or volumes, or hours – not necessarily and perhaps not at all in the language of costs and standards of output so dear to the accountants.

This language barrier suggests that instead of trying to persuade the managers to think in the same terms as the accountants, perhaps accountants should be more ready to lend their experience to interpreting the significance of what they have to tell, by translating it into a variety of languages familiar to many different managers of different disciplines, each one being concerned with his own challenges.

PROPOSITION 4. THAT TRAINING IN BUDGETARY CONTROL MUST BE EFFECTIVE

The fourth proposition was that training in budgetary control must be such that managers attain the level of understanding required. This is of importance even for managers who have both a good educational background and considerable experience in their jobs. It is even more important for managers who lack either or both of these advantages. Such managers may well require a great deal of training in budgetary control if they are to understand it, and to play the part expected of them.

During the course of the R group of studies, comparisons were made between those managers who had received budgetary training and those who had not. The results obtained were as shown in Table 1.9. Some tendency was found for managers who had received training to use their budgets more than managers who had not, but this tendency was not very strong.[1]

---

[1] The value of chi-square obtained is 5·04. With two degrees of freedom, this is not significant at the 5 per cent level (though it is at the 10 per cent level).

However, support for this finding was obtained from the H group of studies. In these studies, 226 managers were asked whether their company's total approach to cost education (including here both formal training and informal advice) had brought about a better understanding of cost systems and the use of cost information for control purposes. 125 said 'no'. Of the 101 managers who said that it had, only 40 identified management training courses outside the company as having been helpful. In-company courses fared rather better, 74 managers stating these to have been of value. The majority (125) of the managers, however, did not consider that they had gained anything from their company's efforts towards cost education. Of the managers who took this view, 85 said they had an inadequate knowledge of costing – and that courses and lectures had not been very helpful in adding to their knowledge. 84 criticised in-company courses and 69 were also critical of external management training. The chief complaint was that training courses, whether inside or outside the company, lost their value because they were not accompanied by help in applying the knowledge gained to everyday situations. The most significant criticism was directed not at the technology of the subject, but at something much more fundamental – inadequate personal contact with the cost accountants.

Table 1.9

RELATIONSHIP BETWEEN TRAINING IN
BUDGETING AND USE MADE OF BUDGETS

Use made of budgets	Managers with training	Managers without training
Full	7	5
Limited	12	23
None	9	29

What managers wanted was not so much formal training as an interpretation service aimed at showing the implications of the cost control information, and the significance of alternative consequential courses of action. This was confirmed in the R group of studies. In these studies, contrasts were made between situations in which accountants provided a regular interpretation service to management and situations in which there was no such service. When the use made of budgets was compared,

it was found that in 27 of the 32 cases in which there was interpretation, the manager concerned made some use of his budgets.
On the other hand, the manager made use of budgets in only
20 of the 53 cases in which interpretation was not provided.

Returning to the H group of studies, these also were notable
for the emphasis placed by managers on the importance of
frequent contact with information producers. Out of 178
managers who were asked what they considered to be the best
way of improving their understanding of cost information, 163
stressed the need for a closer working relationship with accountants who produced the information. Infrequent personal contact was often blamed for failures to appreciate cost information,
and it was argued that accountants would greatly increase their
effectiveness if they became more involved with operations at
shop-floor level.

PROPOSITION 5. THAT INFORMATION PRODUCTION
MUST BE APPROPRIATELY ORGANISED

The fifth proposition was that the organisation of the information flow should be appropriate for the manager who must take
the action.

The relevance for managers of two distinct methods of
organising budgetary control staff was contrasted in the H
group of studies. In eight of the ten companies studied, there
was a centralised organisation. Here, all cost information was
compiled and analysed in a central office, which dispatched
appropriate returns to the departmental managers. The
management accountants might visit the production departments from time to time, but they were based on a central office
and spent nearly all their time there. By contrast, in the other
two companies there was a decentralised organisation with a
cost accountant situated in each of the main production and
service departments advising shop management and carrying
out practical cost training. These two companies did have a
central cost office, but its function was mainly confined to cost
recording, most of the analysis being performed by the departmental accountants.

In these two companies, decentralisation had been carried
out only comparatively recently, so that it was possible to

compare the situation before and after decentralisation. The vast majority of managers considered that their understanding of cost information for control had been enhanced since cost accountants had been located in their departments. Out of 48 managers, 43 took this view and only 5 disagreed. It was also found that the overall cost education efforts of the two companies with decentralised costing organisations were rated as more effective than were the efforts of the other eight companies. While in the eight companies only 63 out of 178 managers thought that these efforts had contributed to better understanding, in the other two companies 38 out of 48 managers held this view. Further, of these 38 managers, 36 attributed the success of cost education to frequent personal contacts with accountants.[1]

This improved understanding arising from personal contact was reflected in the relatively great extent to which departmental information was used by managers, as compared with information produced centrally. In the companies with centralised costing organisations, only 52 out of 178 managers considered cost reports to be a useful tool,[2] while in the companies with decentralised costing organisations 41 out of 48 managers considered cost reports to be useful. Even with a decentralised organisation some cost reports were still produced from a central office, and it was notable that out of the above 48 managers only 10 considered these centrally produced reports to be of value. It seemed that once a decentralised organisation had been instituted, the reports coming from the central cost office were perceived to be too remote and out of touch to be of value as cost control tools.

Specifically, two criticisms were levelled at centrally produced reports. The first of these was that centrally produced reports were less closely geared to the real needs of departmental managers than were reports produced by their departmental accountants. Centrally produced reports often gave equal

[1] An additional advantage claimed for the decentralised form of costing organisation was that by bringing trainee cost clerks into close contact with line managers, it enabled them to understand relatively rapidly the nature of shop-floor management problems. This seemed plausible, but was not subjected to any quantitative test.

[2] In these companies, managers preferred instead to rely on unprocessed data derived from performance reports by shift foremen and from log-books.

attention to all cost items, though the interests of departmental managers would have been better served by concentration on a few critical items. This contrasted with departmental reports, in which accountants located on the spot could highlight variances of special importance at any particular time.

The second criticism was that centrally produced reports were provided at most weekly, and often arrived more than a week after the week to which they referred. A departmental costing organisation enabled accountants to provide information to departmental managers on a daily basis, so that action could be taken while the circumstances which had caused adverse variances were still fresh in mind. 44 out of 48 managers in the two 'decentralised' companies regarded this relatively speedy service as being just as important as the provision of more relevant information.[1]

These findings have deep significance for companies which are involved in the transfer of their control information service to computers.

It has been suggested by Toynbee that the centralisation of all authority may well prove in fact to be the last stage in the decay of a society, which is not its popular interpretation. The centralisation of all information flows may be the analogous kiss of death for effective action by cost-conscious management. This is not to say that information production should not be a process centralised by computers, but operational and management control should not be confused. Where human judgement is concerned, the manager should be in a position to demand immediately, if necessary, the information which he wants, and he must be in a position to know what he wants. The computer was seen long ago as an ideal instrument for decentralisation of management – not the other way round.[2]

The manager may be trained, and in future should be trained, to tap central data banks; or he may rely on his own interpreter, in effect a chief of staff, to do this for him. But to ask him to lose

[1] Another advantage of departmental reports was that their format could be tailored to the views of particular departmental managers. For example, if a departmental manager preferred information to be expressed in physical rather than financial terms, or liked to use graphs and charts, then these individual preferences could be catered for in departmental reports where they could not in centrally produced reports.

[2] J. R. M. Simmons, *Leo and the Managers* (London: Macdonald, 1962).

his own management accountant and to rely instead upon information provided by a distant centralised accounting department, as and when it can do this, may be in effect to remove his eyes and ears and then expect him to be a more effective manager.

PROPOSITION 6. THAT MANAGERS MUST UNDERSTAND THE PURPOSES OF THE BUDGETARY SYSTEM

With any formal process of information production, there is always a danger that the information system will come to be seen as an end in itself. But control information is only of value in so far as it helps managers to take action for the purpose of control. However excellently designed a control information system may be, it will be ineffective unless line managers are willing to co-operate with it. For there to be this co-operation, it is essential that line managers should see the control information system as being there to assist them, and should be willing to become involved with it. The purposes of the control system must be clear to the managers who are expected to exercise control.

The vital issue of the attitudes of line managers towards the cost control information system was explored as part of the H group of studies. In these studies, senior and middle managers were asked to define what they considered to be the main objective of the cost information system. The results obtained are shown in Table 1.10. From this it is clear that there were significant differences of view between the senior and the middle managers.[1]

To 47 of the 54 senior managers it seemed quite clear that the system was intended to provide better control for the middle managers. This was a perfectly clear vision by the senior managers of the cost control information system with respect to their middle managers. 406 middle managers were then asked to state what they considered to be the main objective of the system. 68 thought the main purpose was to cost the product; 60 that it was primarily there to measure the efficiency of

---

[1] The application of a chi-square test confirms the significance of these differences. With four degrees of freedom, a value for chi-square of 88·2 is obtained, which is significant at the 5 per cent level.

operations; 97 that it was indeed intended to be a control tool to help them as managers.

168, however, were of the opinion that the principal purpose of the system of budgetary control was to enable their higher management to check their competence as middle managers. They saw the cost information system as existing to judge them (by measuring their personal efficiency or the efficiency of the operations they supervised) rather than to help them.

Table 1.10

DIFFERING VIEWS AS TO THE MAIN OBJECTIVE OF THE COST INFORMATION SYSTEM

Views as to main objective of system	SENIOR managers	MIDDLE managers
To measure personal efficiency	2	168
To measure the efficiency of operations	2	60
To act as a control tool for the manager	47	97
To assist in product costing	2	68
Don't know	1	13
	54	406

This led many of these managers to have an enormous inbuilt emotional resistance to the whole idea of the budgetary system, which nevertheless they were expected to use for purposes of control. The hostility of middle managers towards the prospect of being judged by the system manifested itself in the form of doubts as to the system's accuracy.[1] Senior and middle managers were asked to estimate the degree of inaccuracy in certain material cost information coming to them from the shop floor via the cost office. The results obtained were as shown in Table 1.11.

Taking the 'over 40 per cent' class as covering a range of 41–80 per cent, arithmetic means are obtained as follows:

	Mean proportion of inaccurate information(%)
Senior managers	17
Middle managers	40

[1] The attitude of foremen who viewed cost control information mainly as a 'pressure device' led also on occasion to deliberate misrecordings of figures. In some cases middle managers knew of this, and it reinforced their general doubts as to the system's accuracy.

The difference between these means is significant at the 5 per cent level.

Over two-thirds of the senior managers thought that these particular figures were accurate to within 20 per cent. On the other hand, over two-thirds of the middle managers thought that the figures were at least 30 per cent inaccurate, and more than one-third that they were more than 40 per cent inaccurate.

Table 1.11

ESTIMATES OF THE DEGREE OF INACCURACY IN MATERIAL
COST INFORMATION COMPILED BY A CENTRAL COST OFFICE
FROM SHOP-FLOOR DATA

Estimate of proportion inaccurate	No. of SENIOR managers making this estimate	No. of MIDDLE managers making this estimate
Less than 20%	23	36
21–30%	9	91
31–40%	4	138
Over 40%	–	141
	36	406

The point was not, of course, who was right and who was wrong, but that there was quite clearly a substantial gulf between the higher and the middle managements' values and beliefs about the budgetary control system's reliability for the purposes for which it was designed.

If a middle manager does not consider that his performance against budget is a fair method of assessing his competence as a manager; if he thinks that it is substantially irrelevant or inappropriate; if he thinks it does not really relate to central issues; or if he suspects the interpretation which his masters will put on the apparent results; then how can he make effective use of budgeting as a system for control?

Part II

This describes the development of the first studies in management accounting to cover a wide range of studies in management control information.

2 Introduction to Broader Studies in Management Control Information

In this chapter the implications are explored of the historical accident by which the accountant captured the management information system. It is argued that accounting information of itself is insufficient to represent the whole area of management concern.

THE BUDGETARY CONTROL SYSTEM

The extraordinary results shown in Chapter 1 must cause the reader to reflect upon the historical accident by which the accountant took responsibility for the production of budgetary control information in the first place. It is possible to argue that accountants, having captured the production of control information, were themselves captured by a fascination with the intricacies of their own discipline. If the management control information system is not effective, this may be because it is viewed too narrowly by accountants, who do not provide the *range* of information required to meet the needs of the managerial situation. Accountants have been either unwilling or unable to come to grips with these needs.

Thus the challenges may lie not so much in accounting as in other fields, for example in the values and attitudes of those who are in authority, or in the nature of the relationships of the different managers within the organisation.

We are entitled to ask, then, whether the budgetary control system with all its ramifications, its feet in work study and in scientific standards, and its super-structure of longer-term planning and budgets, is inherently a suitable kind of control system for executive managers.

If it is, what is required to ensure that it does meet managements' needs and requirements, to ensure that it is effective as a control system? What do we mean by an effective system? If the budgetary control system is not appropriate for managements' purposes, why not, and what can be done about it?

The great merit of the hieroglyphics used by accountants, in which they express their information, is that this is a form of language into which all sorts of information can be translated. Accountants have done more than any other professional body to develop and advance sophisticated systems for the receipt, translation and production of information for managers. Their efforts are entitled to respect. It is as a consequence of their having done more than anyone else in this field of management information that they are more open than anyone else to criticism.

Accountants were the first to provide management with formal and written information about the business. Their rules are arbitrary. For their purposes of measurement and of recording, accountants have adopted a number of conventions. These are artificial, and have to be learned. They are understood by accountants in companies all over the world, but nevertheless the rules are arbitrary.

Under the influences of the Inland Revenue, of the Companies Acts, and of the necessity for compliance with other statutory requirements, accountants produce all kinds of information from their records, and analyse certain parts of it as they are directed or inclined to do. Their systems are, by any criteria, advanced, reliable and invaluable, and the information so provided is universally clear, at least to the accountants.

But at all times the pressure on the accountant is to produce information for interests which are external to the management, e.g. information for the benefit of the shareholders, for the creditors of the company, for would-be investors, for the benefit of banks and the money market, for the company's suppliers.

When the enterprise was small and management was synonymous with ownership, or the manager was so close to the activities of the enterprise that he could rely primarily on informal communications systems, only a fraction of the information on which he acted and managed his business was necessarily presented to him in a formal way. The complexity and diversity and the sheer scale of the industrial organisation today means that managers necessarily are guided more by reference to budgets and plans, and have to sift through masses of statements about all sorts of subjects in connection with the business.

Central to this whole flow of facts and figures to the managers is the accountants' information. It was the engineer with precise standards in physical terms, able to determine exactly the sequence of events leading to the final product, with agreed tolerances and degrees of deviation from planned performance, who taught the accountant to convert his standards to standards of cost, and to set equivalent standards for all other expenditure, and then for income too.

This standard cost and budgetary control system, so widely developed in industrial organisations, may for convenience be determined the 'conventional' system.

Management is now given a profit and loss account, showing sales compared with budgeted or target sales, costs compared with budgeted costs, with analyses of differences, etc., this information being summarised for higher management. The summaries are underpinned by a hierarchy of subordinate returns designed for different levels of management right down to labour and output summaries for the foremen on the shop floor.

This budgetary control system has been designed by the accountants not for interests external to the business, but for the managers. It is hoped that it will enable management to manage their part of the business more effectively. In theory, it is a control tool of immense significance, capable, if properly understood and properly used, of providing management at every level with a very powerful aid to more effective management.

But are the terms in which performance is measured by accountants the terms in which the managers measure their performance? How can this system, which is potentially so valuable, be so developed that management will respect it and rely upon it? Many managers evidently do not do this at present, and it can hardly be assumed that this is all the fault of the management. How can those who design so powerful a tool for managers be sure that the managers will in fact use it, or will use it for the purpose which the designers had in mind?

THE ACCOUNTANT AND MANAGEMENT INFORMATION

By historical accident arising from his role as the custodian of the vital financial information, the accountant has in effect captured the management information system. As a result it is widely and commonly assumed that the form in which the accountant presents information, and even the subjects selected for such presentation, are necessarily appropriate for the management; that this is the right kind of formal information system; that it contains the quintessence of all that a manager needs to know in order to determine the progress of his department.

But management cannot and does not disregard an immense number of aspects of his department which are outside the vision, apparently, of the specialists who designed his returns.

If someone with an entirely different set of values, a sociologist, for example, or a psychologist, or a doctor, were asked to examine a department, and select those features in it which he would consider to be most important, and to deserve critical study and a flow of up-to-date information, he might select entirely different aspects, by contrast with those regarded as most important by the accountants; and we cannot say that attention to such things would not have value, or lead to higher performance figures, even measured in conventional profit and loss. A doctor might point to the unfortunate effects on output or behaviour of a poor diet. A psychologist might analyse the decision-making processes, and such analysis might reveal dramatic effects on output of the employees' lack of control over their work.

It is not to be assumed that the interests of the accountants are necessarily the most important or significant, even for results measured in economic terms; or that these are the features which the management should watch and control in order to improve results, however measured.

Moreover, the features where performance is critical for results today will no doubt be different tomorrow. The information system must be prepared to meet such changing requirements.

The critical features for the different levels and kinds of management can perhaps be identified by reference to the minimum achievement needs of the firm as a whole. Where achievement is critical, information is vital.

Critical for what? Presumably for achievement, for success, for successful management. If the manager does not know what will be regarded by his superiors as successful management, and what will be regarded in him as failure, then he is likely to come to his own conclusions about these things, possibly the wrong conclusions. He may believe, for example, that his main task is to maintain morale, while his superiors think that it is to cut costs.

What value will the manager attach to an information system which is not designed to provide information about those things which he knows or believes to matter the most, or which does not reflect his own sense of achievement? In practice, with or without reference to a formal information system, managers receive all kinds of information, on all sorts of subjects, through a great variety of channels, and as a result of experience they attempt to identify the most significant features of their information, and to react accordingly.

In smaller organisations the informal information system may be more important for day-to-day management than formally produced figures. In larger organisations, formal information is in practice produced for executive management by a wide variety of personnel and on a wide variety of topics.

In such large organisations, managers must in practice largely depend on their formal control information, and this dependence may have far-reaching implications, both for the features which the managers try to control and also how they try to control them.

It may be argued that the function of control information is to provide comparisons of achieved results with desired goals. If in some particular the performance achieved is shown to have fallen away from the performance desired, the need for management attention and correction becomes apparent. Thus control information must be provided for managers in such a form and at such a time that the managers can rely upon it. Moreover, there must be managerial agreement as to those aspects of the enterprise which currently are of critical importance, and the control information provided must concentrate on these critical aspects.

Critical then for what? What, indeed, is successful management? This question can hardly be answered for any individual or group of managers, without reference to the purposes and constraints of the enterprise as a whole; and then the purposes of the particular departments or sections with their part to play in the achievement of enterprise purposes; and then the role of the manager himself, in his capacity as a manager.

MANUFACTURING COMPANIES: OBJECTIVES AND INFORMATION NEEDS

The purposes of a manufacturing organisation are manifold, but clearly some purposes are more important than others. According to one point of view, there can only be one central dominant objective – for example, the unconditional surrender of the enemy – all other purposes being subordinate. Their attainment will eliminate the constraints which deter the achievement of the central purpose. Other objectives are only legitimate in so far as their achievement would further the achievement of the central purpose.

There are alternative views. It has been suggested[1] that the objectives of the firm should be derived by balancing conflicting aims, i.e. the claims of the various stakeholders in the firm – the managers, workers, stockholders, suppliers and vendors. The firm has responsibility to all of these and it must arrange its objectives so as to give each a measure of satisfaction. Each group of participants possesses certain interests, and negotiations are required to establish a set of acceptable objectives such that, by a coalition of these different interests, the operation of the firm can continue. Under this so-called 'stakeholder' theory, the established objectives must be renegotiated from time to time, in response to changes in the industrial environment, or in the internal power position of the different groups. Each group will necessarily be interested in different aspects of performance –

---

[1] H. I. Ansoff, *Corporate Strategy* (New York: McGraw-Hill, 1965) p. 39.

shareholders, for example, in dividends and capital appreciation, employees in conditions and career opportuniites, and
the interests of given groups will change according to the
circumstances under which the firm operates.[1]

Whether the higher management conceives that there is one
central purpose and all others are subordinate and peripheral
purposes, or whether there are a variety of purposes of some
merit which have to be balanced in some manner, it is clear that
every manufacturing company has certain minimum needs.
There are some areas in which every manufacturing company
must achieve certain results if it is to survive.

The conventional system of management control depends
upon an examination of variances in performance which are
measured by reference to predetermined budgets, or standards.
Management control has been loosely defined as the process by
which managers ensure that resources are obtained and used
effectively and efficiently in the accomplishment of the
organisation's, or firm's, objectives. The firm for this purpose
may be considered to be an open system, which operates within
the larger system of its environment. The firm's own system
may be thus visualised as consisting of a number of subsystems
which are interrelated, each subsystem having its own objectives
whose combined achievement should lead to the attainment of
the firm's ultimate purposes. This approach stresses the need to
identify objectives and to establish subsystems in which satisfactory performance is seen to be critically important. Management control is thus concerned with the maintenance within
allowable and predetermined limits of the performance which is
required if the purposes of the firm are to be achieved.

Because the critical subsystems of corporate activity have
been identified in the main by accountants, the measures most
commonly found in the control system are those expressed in
accounting terms. Management control systems everywhere are
in the process of evolution, but they have nowhere yet entirely
escaped the conventions of accounting practice. And here lies

[1] For example, the interests of managers as a group may vary from a
desire to ensure corporate survival in periods of strain to a wish to carry out
creative activity when business conditions are favourable enough for a
diversion of resources to activities which do not immediately contribute to
profitability.

a fundamental difficulty. These conventions have evolved along lines which are essentially of interest to accountants. They were never designed for the convenience of managers. As such, they may be inappropriate, while there is evidence that, even if appropriate, they are not well understood by the managers who are expected to interpret them.

Accountants demand a certain measure of objectivity arising from their traditional function of stewardship of corporate assets. The tendency is to rely on historically precise records of past events, and on traditional measures.

It is clear that expenditure, for example, on research and development, on employee welfare, on management training, or on advertising, is likely to create assets for the firm. These assets may be in terms of new products or better employee relations, or increased sales, or improved management performance. The creation of such assets may even be vitally necessary if profits are to be made in the future.

But because the value of such assets is extremely difficult to measure, accountants prefer to consider the expenditures which create these assets simply as current costs, and to write off such expenditure in the accounting period in which it was incurred. They confine their attention to the valuation of more tangible assets. This attitude, while it preserves their notion of objectivity largely intact, has the disadvantage of making accounting profits at best a very short-term measure of business success.

So for this reason again a control system based purely upon control of the constituents of accounting profit is likely to exclude variables required for successful control, where progress may be essential for the long-term interests of the business.

At one time, all information was regarded as inherently confidential, if not indeed the secret of top management. Something of this attitude may still linger here and there. If managers are not well informed, they can hardly be expected to decide more than some fraction of their department's, or indeed of their own, information requirements.

Management in practice must largely be aware of the critical aspects of the business, and of the need for investment in a variety of ways, whether or not such investments are measured by the conventional system.

The manager is inevitably concerned to watch progress in a

variety of vitally important areas, whether accountants measure or ignore them, and to that extent to control development.

The manager should therefore consider his information requirements with care: it is for him to decide the system and for it to meet his needs. Does it do so?

3 Management Control Reports

This chapter describes the scope of the first group of studies in control information.

MANAGEMENT AND CONTROL

By some standards, the management accountants' system is as yet only in the very early stages of its development as a management control and information system. Managers must in practice still largely depend on information outside this conventional system.

A great variety of information is now necessarily prepared formally and presented in written form. Such information should enable management to monitor performance comprehensively. Management should be able to obtain from this great variety of information an indication of those activities which seem to deserve special attention at any given time, or confirmation that progress in all fields is in accordance with what is required, readily seeing any deviations, with some indication of their significance.

Formal control information in large complex organisations is produced in ever-larger volumes every day. But to what extent is this control information relevant and appropriate for managements' purposes?

Can it be assumed that management is thereby given a clear view of the critically important activities, and that the information which is provided to managers for control purposes is appropriate to their needs?

These research studies on management control information were based originally on the budgetary control information prepared by management accountants. They revealed a high degree of managerial indifference towards this information.

The findings raised questions which went far beyond the information system of the accountants, being concerned with the whole flow of information provided to managers, upon which their management might largely be expected to depend.

It was decided therefore to take a look at the whole range of formal written reports which are provided to the managements of substantial industrial enterprises for control purposes.

THE FOCUS ON MANUFACTURING

It was not possible or necessary to search for firms which might be representative of the whole of British industry. It was decided therefore to study in the first instance seven companies, all engaged in manufacturing, not in any way interconnected, and not in any way related to the companies in which the studies in budgetary control had been undertaken.

Why manufacturing companies exclusively? In some respects the management control problems of commercial firms, of manufacturing firms and of non-commercial organisations present similar images and lend themselves to similar approaches. But the control of non-manufacturing organisations often requires complex ways of measuring performance, and these research studies had to be undertaken within the time available for their completion. Moreover, the purposes of non-manufacturing organisations will differ substantially by comparison with those of manufacturing companies. We wanted to look at a number of organisations whose purposes and requirements for minimum achievement would not be too widely dissimilar.[1]

For this reason, we also found it convenient to exclude retailing organisations, because the variables which must be controlled in retailing are not the same as those which must be

---

[1] 'When the outputs are services or other intangibles, the problem of measuring them becomes formidable; it is always difficult and often not feasible to measure the output of hospitals, schools, government agencies or churches.' See J. S. Hekimian, *Management Control in Life Insurance Branch Offices* (Cambridge, Mass.: Harvard U.P., 1965) p. 3.

controlled for successful manufacturing.[1] For this reason also, companies in service industries were disregarded.[2] Although in any one field for control, say in the financial field, such differences would be tolerable and could be catered for, the intention of these studies was to take a look at the formal information system as a whole from the point of view of the manager who has to exercise the control.

THE INFORMATION

The interest was to be concentrated on control reports, defined for these purposes as documents which stated performance and met the following requirements:

1. Having a fixed format and/or typographical layout.
2. Presented at regular intervals.
3. To a specified manager or group of managers.
4. For purposes of comparison.

Such reports are issued regularly in all substantial companies, by various departments, and are provided for different levels of management on a variety of subjects, from hours lost by absenteeism in the foundries to value of sales in Mexico – the first possibly appearing on a report from the personnel department, the second perhaps from the sales department.

The yardstick for comparison purposes might be shown within the report, e.g. by reference to budget or predetermined standards, or to performance at some other time, or it might not be so stated but it might be found by reference to another document. The comparison might be on the report itself, or it might be left to the manager to make his own comparison.

---

[1] A detailed description of the nature of these differences is to be found in E. A. Helfert, E. G. May and M. P. McNair, *Controllership in Department Stores* (Cambridge, Mass.: Harvard U.P., 1965) p. 25.

[2] This is recognised by Stokes, who, in an appendix to his book on management control, gives lists of the items of control information produced by three companies, one in manufacturing and the other two in service industries. Very few of the non-monetary items of control information quoted are common to all three companies. See P. M. Stokes, *A Total Systems Approach to Management Control* (New York: American Management Association, 1968) pp. 140–53.

THE MANAGEMENT

The focus of these studies was to be on the manager, on the values he attached to his control information, and on his reasons for reliance on, or neglect of, this information. The purposes which he may have had in mind, and the ways in which his information may have affected his decisions, although of great interest, were not the central subject of these studies.

The manager, for these purposes, was either a senior executive immediately responsible to a member of the board of directors, or an executive responsible to that senior manager – the middle manager, so termed. There was no reason why members of the board should be omitted, other than the assumption that they are concentrating on matters of policy and strategy, and with the longer term, while control is associated with the middle levels of management for whom strategy and policy are given, at least in theory.[1] Managers below the board are expected to concern themselves with the translation of policy into action, and with the making and implementation of day-to-day decisions. For such purposes, middle managers commonly and regularly receive control information.

The attention given in these studies to the senior manager was subordinate to the attention paid to the middle manager. Indeed, the studies at senior levels were intended to throw light on the middle manager, who is so often charged with lonely and massive responsibilities in the front trenches of the battle, and who it is expected both can and will produce the results which his senior executives want.

KEY RESULT AREAS

For purposes of convenience, it was necessary to sort the masses of control information provided into classes or categories, and for this purpose a commonly discussed classification was

[1] The irrelevance to the board of control reports covering relatively short periods is expressed by Juran and Louden as follows: 'The current month's performance is not that important to the Board. It is not the basis for changing the program, passing the dividend, writing a policy, or any other board action.' See J. M. Juran and J. K. Louden, *The Corporate Director* (New York: American Management Association, 1966) p. 146.

adopted – the so-called 'key result areas'. The theory behind these is simply that all manufacturing companies have in common a number of critical interests in the sense that a failure in any one of these would effectively prevent the advance of the company in a competitive economy, even though results in all the other areas were satisfactory.[1]

The original selection has been checked several times independently, both by practising managers and by academics. All of them reached quite similar conclusions as to these key result areas, which have also been found valid in economies as far apart as those of the United States and Soviet Russia. Moreover, they are common knowledge, so that it was convenient to adopt them as the framework for these first broader studies of the control information provided for middle management.

In theory, information on key aspects of management performance should be collated, and the results should be reflected in the management control reporting system.

The information provided for management in their control reports was first arranged, therefore, under the following headings:

1. Market standing.
2. Innovation.
3. Productivity.
4. Physical resources.
5. Financial resources.
6. (Current) profitability.
7. Manager performance and development.
8. Worker performance and attitude.
9. Public responsibility.

All the control information[2] provided for the middle managers

[1] Probably the first company to go on record with a public list of their key result areas was G.E.C. in America; see *Planning, Managing and Measuring the Business* (New York: Controllership Foundation, 1955) p. 30. Another early approach is to be found in *Management Planning and Control: The H. J. Heinz Approach* (New York: Financial Executives Research Foundation, 1957) esp. pp. 95–7. More recent studies include E. C. Miller, *Objectives and Standards: An Approach to Planning and Control*, Research Study No. 74 (New York: American Management Association, 1966), and Stokes, op. cit.

[2] An item of control information is here defined as a unit of data which

was assigned to one or other of these broad performance areas.

Of course, some items of information could arguably be included in several categories; for example, 'labour turnover' has relevance both for productivity and for labour attitudes. But as these categories are for convenience only, the information was assigned to one or other of these areas on the basis of company practice and common sense, e.g.:

1. *Market standing.* Items measuring the firm's competitive position in the sales of its products, including sales volume, market share, and volume of orders.

2. *Innovation.* Items measuring the development of new products or processes, including the costs of research and development.

3. *Productivity.* Items measuring the efficiency with which inputs to the production processes were converted into outputs, including production volume variances, labour efficiencies and raw material consumption variances.

4. *Physical resources.* Items measuring the volume or value of physical inputs, including labour hours worked and raw material price variances.

5. *Financial resources.* Such items as bank balances, overdue payments, progress of capital expenditure against budget.

6. *Profitability.* Items measuring profit either as an absolute value or as a return on the capital employed.

7. *Manager performance and development.* Such items as personal merit ratings, promotions, attendance on training courses.

8. *Worker performance and attitude.* Such items as individual or group output or bonus figures, rates of labour turnover, days lost through absenteeism, and also such expenditures as operative education, welfare and training.

9. *Public responsibility.* Items referring to the cost or effectiveness of public relations activities.

---

represents performance on a particular subject, and which is produced at regular intervals, e.g. a weekly statement of the value of sales would be classified as an item of control information, and since it summarises sales revenue performance, it would be assigned to the key result area of market standing.

THE COMPANIES STUDIED: FIRST STAGE

The companies selected ranged widely in size, and were chosen
from very different industries:

Company	Industry	No. of employees
A	Fibre products	3500
B	Abrasives	900
C	Diesel engines	2200
D	Cars	4500
E	Paints	800
F	Batteries	1100
G	Storage radiators	400

4 Preliminary Findings

The purpose of this chapter is to present the results of this wider study by the authors, which examined within a key result area framework:

1. The use made of management control information generally.
2. The reasons why a great deal of this information is not used.

As much as 46 per cent of the control information produced was found not to be used, thus underlining the significance of the problem.

THE USE OF INFORMATION

In each of these seven companies, the first research studies lasted approximately six weeks, and involved in all 129 personal interviews with responsible personnel at management level.[1] Of these, 65 were functionally responsible for the production of control information to line managers, but as senior functional staff they were themselves managers in the sense that they managed their own staff departments. For present purposes they will therefore be called 'staff', in order to distinguish them from the 64 interviewees who were the executive or line managers at middle management levels, and who for ease of reference will be termed 'managers'.

Hundreds (579) of items of control information[2] were considered in these studies and discussed with the managers. The

[1] A classification of the managers interviewed by function is to be found in Appendix A.

[2] It should be noted that a control report may contain more than one item of control information. For example, if a report contained information both on sales revenue and selling expenses, that report would be said to contain two separate items of control information.

findings of the interviews with the 64 line managers are illustrated in Table 4.1.[1]

Of the 579 items of control information, 267 or 46 per cent

Table 4.1

THE USE MADE OF CONTROL INFORMATION

Key result area	No. of items of which substantial use was made	No. of items considered to be irrelevant or background information
Innovation	17	14
Productivity	80	80
Physical resources	65	58
Market standing	87	51
Financial resources	14	11
Profitability	12	14
Worker performance and attitude	33	38
Manager performance and development	4	1
	312	267

Note: There were 16 items of control information for which the answers given relating to use were insufficiently clear for classification. The 3 items encountered relating to public responsibility all fell into this category.

[1] Before discussing these findings, a point must be made about how they were obtained. In order to summarise, it was necessary to add the findings from different managers. The method adopted can best be illustrated by an example. Suppose two production managers were interviewed, one of whom received 6 items of control information while the other received 7; then the total number of items received by them together would be 13. If the first manager used 4 of his 6 items, while the second used 2 of his 7, then the total number of items of information used by the two together would be 6. Thus it could be said that, of the 13 items received by the two managers, 6 were used. This would be tabulated as follows:

Function of managers interviewed	No. of items of which substantial use was made	No. of items considered to be irrelevant or background information
Production	6	7

In analysing the findings, key result areas were used as a basis of classification of the subjects covered in a control report, and items of control information were assigned to key result areas in accordance with the principles outlined.

were regarded by the line managers as irrelevant, or at best to be simply background information, sometimes but not necessarily of any interest.

Of course, some control information is produced for managers specifically because it provides useful background information. Nevertheless, a considerable waste of time is implied in the finding that the managers in fact made little or no use of almost half of all the control information which they were given.[1]

This conclusion is the more striking when it is remembered that it is only companies with relatively progressive managements which are willing to provide research facilities, and are sufficiently interested to allow such studies as these.

Detailed study of Table 4.1. provides further interest. Not only was a high proportion of all these items of information not used by the line managers for control purposes, but the proportion which was not used varied very little between the key result areas under which the information had been analysed. Statistical tests showed the variation not to be significant. Moreover, there was no significant variation when the data were reclassified by the function of the managers receiving the control information, e.g. production, sales, etc., rather than by key result areas.

The line managers over all the range and variety of activities appeared to have the same problem, namely that a high proportion of the control information they received was of little or no use to them. Of course, substantially more information was produced on some key result areas than on others, but the

---

[1] In a further investigation (reported in more detail in Chapter 7) the authors asked 49 middle managers in five different companies to classify the items of control information they received into:

1. Vital: items for which even a slight delay in production or inaccuracy in content would be a matter of immediate personal concern.
2. Important: items to which reference is often made but which, if delayed or inaccurate, would not make effective management impossible.
3. Background: items to which reference is rarely, if ever, made.

Out of 483 items, 153 (32 per cent) were considered vital, 173 (36 per cent) important, and 157 (32 per cent) background. Thus even with a more stringent definition, nearly one-third of the items on their control reports fell into the category of unimportant background information.

reasons for non-use were apparently not related to management concern with one key result area as opposed to another.

To what could such non-use be attributed?

REASONS FOR NON-USE

(a) Out of Time

A major reason given by the line managers was that information was received so long after the period to which it related that it was no longer a guide to effective action. For brevity, this information will be described as 'untimely'.

In the original management accounting studies, no fewer than 150 out of 152 managers described their cost information as arriving too late for it to serve any useful purpose, but in these studies, concerned with all kinds of control information analysed under different subjects, the relative importance of untimeliness as a reason for non-use was found to vary significantly from one key result area to another (Table 4.2).

Table 4.2

ITEMS OF CONTROL INFORMATION NOT USED BECAUSE THEY
WERE PRODUCED TOO SLOWLY

Key result area	No. of items arriving too late for effective action	No. of items arriving quickly enough but not used for other reasons
Worker performance and attitude	6	30
Market standing	9	38
Innovation	4	9
Physical resources	21	36
Profitability and financial resources	10	15
Productivity	30	43
	80	171

Note: There were 16 items of control information concerning which the
      evidence obtained was insufficiently clear for classification as above.
      The 3 items encountered relating to public responsibility all fell into
      this category.

Lack of timeliness appeared to be an important reason for non-use in the more conventional key result areas of productivity, physical resources, profitability and financial resources. In these, timeliness of control information was considered to be critical.[1]

By contrast, timeliness of information was thought to be less important in the areas of market standing, innovation, and worker performance and attitude.

In these areas, it was often not clear what level of performance would be considered sufficiently unsatisfactory to warrant remedial action. Hence there was less pressure to report performance quickly. Subsequent evidence from other studies suggested that in these more recently recognised areas it was thought to be comparatively difficult to establish standards of satisfactory performance, and that less attention had been given to standards.

(b) Other

There appeared to be four other major reasons for managements' failure to use their information for control purposes. The relative importance of these reasons, by contrast with the reason of untimeliness, did not seem to differ significantly from one result area to another. In order of importance, these four reasons for non-use were:

1. The subjects on which the information was provided were outside the control of the managers.
2. The information which was provided was insufficiently detailed to be helpful.
3. The information was considered to be inaccurate.
4. The information was not presented in a form which could be readily understood.

Again, one can observe the same kinds of reasons and the same tendencies as appeared when management accounting information was first studied.

The relative importance of each of these reasons is illustrated in Table 4.3

[1] In Table 4.2, for the purpose of statistical analysis, the key result areas of profitability and financial resources have been amalgamated into a single key result area. For the same reason, the one item of control information concerning manager performance and development that was said to be irrelevant has been included with worker performance and attitude.

Two reasons evidently dominated the rest and accounted for two-thirds of the information which managers did not use. Of roughly equal importance to untimeliness, already mentioned, was that the subjects on which the information was provided were outside the control of the managers.

Table 4.3

THE DEFECTS OF ITEMS OF CONTROL INFORMATION
WHICH WERE NOT USED

Reasons for non-use	*No. of items not used for this reason*
Subjects covered outside managers' control	85
Arrives too late for effective action	80
Insufficient detail provided	31
Thought to be inaccurate	25
Not provided in a form that can be understood	10
Other reasons	20
	251

Such a situation may arise in several ways. The information producers (staff) may fail to understand the nature of the line managers' jobs. They may thus provide information which is not relevant for what the middle managers consider to be their important activities.[1]

Alternatively, the middle managers themselves might not be in agreement with their own line superiors as to the critical aspects of their own jobs. The information received by the middle managers might then reflect the views of higher executives as to what was critical rather than their own executive views.

Any such differences of view between the middle managers and either the staff or their own superior line managers as to the critical features of their jobs would involve differences as to the success criteria to be applied, directly or indirectly, in judging managements' performance.

[1] If this possibility were valid, it might be expected that information producers would provide excessively detailed information on a number of subjects which they considered more important than did middle managers. In fact, excessively detailed information was an extremely rare problem, with only 3 complaints of excessive detail as compared with 31 complaints of inadequate detail.

Could such differences be fundamental to the indifference displayed by the middle managers towards much of the control information with which they were provided?

SUCCESS CRITERIA

This possibility made it especially important to concentrate some studies on the extent to which the functional staff and senior and middle managers were found in practice to be in agreement as to the success criteria to be applied in judging management performance.

It was decided to obtain and to compare, in several companies, the results of studies of these revealing questions, i.e.:

1. The views of the senior managers as to the success criteria of their immediate subordinates' jobs.
2. The views of these subordinates, i.e. the middle managers.
3. The views of the staff (information producers) as to the success criteria of the middle managers to whom they supplied substantial volumes of control information.

For these detailed studies of managers' success criteria, a further five companies were selected. These were not in any way connected with any of the companies which had been previously examined. Moreover, they were deliberately chosen from different industries again.

Chapter 5 will be devoted to the detailed methods used to obtain and to compare the success criteria of the managers. Chapter 6 will provide an analysis of the results of these studies.

5 Middle Management Success Criteria

This chapter begins with a description of the managers and companies examined in the second stage of the study. This is followed by an explanation of the methods used to obtain managers' views concerning success criteria. At the end of the chapter there is an outline of the way in which comparisons were made of these views.

INTRODUCTION

It might be inferred from studies already described that if senior and middle management were not agreed about the criteria of judgement for deciding whether or not the middle management was successful, then it could hardly be expected that the management would be found to be in agreement about the relative worth of the different items of control information supplied, in theory for middle managements' purposes.

Possible relationships between managements' ranking of success criteria, and their ranking in order of importance of items of middle management control information, now deserved some examination. Before doing this it was necessary, however, to see to what extent senior and middle managements agreed as to the proper ways of judging middle managements' performance, i.e. whether and to what extent they ranked middle management criteria in a similar order.

For this purpose, five medium-sized companies, not hitherto studied or in any way related to companies already studied, were selected from five different industries.

The intention being to examine relationships in some depth, this group of studies was somewhat narrower in scope than the first group. In the first group a wide range of managers had been included as typical recipients of control information, including personnel, production control and research managers.

In the new group of studies, the senior managers were selected as before, as being immediately below the level of the board of directors. But the middle managers who responded to these senior managers were only selected for study if they were accustomed to receiving a substantial volume of formal control information – in practice, not fewer than five items on a regular basis.

This group of studies included 150 interviews with line managers or staff managers. All the line managers were involved in production or in sales, as no other groups of managers were found to be in regular receipt of a volume of management control information[1] large enough to satisfy the comparative needs of these studies. Of the 54 staff who produced control information, only 21 were found to be in a position to form judgements about the line managers' success criteria.

The identification and ranking of success criteria for particular middle management jobs in these five companies, therefore, was finally undertaken with 26 senior line managers, 49 middle line managers and 54 staff.[2]

THE COMPANIES STUDIED: SECOND STAGE

The five companies included in this study group for a more detailed examination of success criteria and management information are coded H–M. They were engaged in the following industries and had the following number of employees:

[1] Such managers might well be in receipt of much technical or scientific information about their processes, but operational and management controls are, of course, to be distinguished. See R. N. Anthony, *Planning and Control Systems: A Framework for Analysis* (Cambridge, Mass.: Division of Research, Graduate School of Business Administration, Harvard University, 1965) chap. 1.

[2] The 21 staff who gave judgements about line managers' success criteria were interviewed twice, and the other 33 staff once each. Full details of the scope of this, including a breakdown by function of the managers interviewed, are to be found in Appendix B.

Company	Industry	No. of employees
H	Gear manufacture	3500
J	Warp knitting	1000
K	Yarn processing	2700
L	Weaving	2000
M	Printing machinery	1750

They differed widely in almost every way. Companies J, K and L were in continuous production. Company H produced on a one-off basis. Company M covered the whole spectrum from continuous production to one-off.

There were differences in the supply position, both for labour and for raw materials. Companies H and M faced shortages of both. Company L had serious labour problems but experienced few difficulties in materials supply. Company K was in the reverse position. Company J alone had no significant problems with either labour or materials.

All these companies faced similar market problems. During the period 1969–70 when the studies were undertaken, a severe credit squeeze was in progress. Profit margins were under pressure. Companies J and L were making losses. Company M was just breaking even. The profits of companies H and K had suffered setbacks.

For all the companies, competition was becoming more severe. This had involved companies J, K and L in relatively short runs of technically difficult products with low margins. Company K's problems were aggravated by its dependence on a single product, yet despite this handicap it had largely avoided the short-time working which had been necessary in companies J and L. By contrast, companies H and M were obtaining a very high capacity utilisation, though without correspondingly high profits.

The companies responded in different ways to these problems. Company H was primarily concerned with variety reduction and the elimination of unprofitable lines. At the other extreme, company M was carrying out a major diversification programme aimed at penetrating entirely new markets. Between these extremes came companies J, K and L. The emphasis in company K was on new products. In company J the strategy was to sell the existing products in new (overseas) markets. Company

L's basic approach was to close a number of factories and to concentrate production on a few sites, with ultra-modern machinery. This policy was being followed to a lesser degree by company J.

These differences of approach were in part a reflection of differing degrees of managerial sophistication. Company K was probably the most sophisticated. It had introduced a management by objectives system, had comprehensive standards of cost produced by computer and an excellent reputation for its marketing. Companies J and L were also fairly advanced. Both had established standards of costs, both engaged (as did company K) in long-range planning, both had well-established computer installations. Companies H and M also had computers, but their work was confined to more elementary routines. Company H was noted for its engineering rather than its managerial expertise. It had paid no great attention to management techniques as such. Budgeting and standard costing were both rather primitive, but even so more developed than they were in company M. In many ways company M was the least sophisticated, combining acute production control problems with a slow and inaccurate stock control system.

To summarise, the companies selected differed in their technology, their organisation and their strategy. They faced not dissimilar market problems, but they tackled them in different ways, reflecting differences both in techniques and in outlook.

It was to be expected that the higher management in these companies would see the success criteria of their middle managements' jobs from different viewpoints. It should be emphasised that these studies were not concerned, however, with comparisons between companies, but with comparisons between different levels of management within each company.

METHOD OF OBTAINING SUCCESS CRITERIA

When managers were first asked in simple terms to describe their understanding of the criteria which applied to their jobs, they often found it difficult. They were sometimes quite unable to attempt a concise or comprehensive statement.

A device was therefore introduced to stimulate thought

during the interview without unduly influencing the nature of
the reply.

Two lists were prepared, each with eight possible success
criteria, one list for production management jobs and the other
for sales management jobs. After the manager had attempted to
describe his appropriate criteria he was then asked in a second
question to select from the suggested list those criteria (if any)
which seemed to him to be relevant, whether or not they had
already been discussed.

It seemed likely that the answer given might be influenced
by two considerations. One of these was the method of presentation. If the criteria were presented as a list, undue attention
might be given to the first criterion. Each item was therefore
entered on a separate 9×6 cm card. These 'prompting cards'
were identical to cards on which the research team wrote each
answer to the first question.

Another influence might be the nature of the criteria which
were suggested. A variety of standard works on job descriptions
were therefore checked to ensure that the criteria would relate
to the most commonly encountered areas of responsibility for
production and sales managers.[1]

In addition, the information gained in the first studies was
employed, and the success criteria which were finally selected
were as follows:

Success Criteria for Production Managers

   1. Produce to production schedules.
   2. Meet quality standards.
   3. Keep straight-time labour costs within budget.
   4. Minimise unexpected down-time.
   5. Watch lateness, absenteeism and labour turnover.

---

[1] The works examined in most detail were:

For production managers: G. H. Evans, *Managerial Job Descriptions in
Manufacturing*, Research Study No. 65 (New York: American Management
Association, 1964); E. C. Miller, *Objectives and Standards of Performance in
Production Management*, Research Study No. 84 (New York: American
Management Association, 1967).

For sales managers: JoAnn Sperling, *Job Descriptions in Marketing Manage-
ment* (New York: American Marketing Association, 1969); E. C. Miller,
Objectives and Standards of Performance in Marketing Management, Research
Study No. 85 (New York: American Management Association, 1967).

6. Minimise frequency and severity of accidents.
7. Cut down material waste or scrap.
8. Control overtime.

Success Criteria for Sales Managers
1. Obtain accurate sales forecasts.
2. Achieve budgeted volume of sales.
3. Maintain margins at budgeted level.
4. Increase efficiency of representatives.
5. Obtain favourable public relations.
6. Keep selling costs within budget.
7. Develop new markets.
8. Predict competitors' activities.

The managers interviewed subsequently confirmed that they considered that these criteria on the cards covered the most important aspects of their jobs.

It might be argued that in suggesting criteria to managers with the aid of prompting cards the authors were using a method which might well lead to the appearance of a higher degree of agreement between the managers than in fact existed. This would be a rather difficult proposition to test, because without the prompting cards it was found to be almost impossible to obtain from many managers any clear explanation of their success criteria. If, however, there was any tendency to arrive at a slightly exaggerated degree of agreement on the criteria, because the same prompting cards were used for all the production managers, and the same cards for all the sales managers, then the lack of agreement which was found in a large number of cases becomes of even greater significance.

It can at least be said that the use of prompting cards was consistent with the policy, applied throughout these studies, of producing a conservative estimate of the extent of any disagreement between the managers as to the criteria of successful middle management.

The first two questions thus led to the production of a number of cards, each bearing a brief description of a criterion which the manager concerned thought applicable to a particular middle management job. The senior manager, the middle manager or staff information producer under interview was then asked to rank these criteria. He was asked to put these in the order of the importance he attached to each for the middle management job under examination.

Thus, the manager could look at the cards with the criteria he had identified spontaneously, and if one of these had been inappropriately described, he had the opportunity to say so.

The manager also had to manipulate the cards, to place them in an order. Several commented that this process compelled them to think hard and more clearly.

The views of senior managers, middle managers and information producers on the success criteria of particular middle management jobs were thus collected separately.

DERIVATION OF MANAGEMENT PAIRS

Having thus collected these management opinions, the next step was to compare them; and these comparisons were made in pairs. For example, if a senior manager and his immediate subordinate had each been asked for the success criteria of the subordinate's job, the answers of this pair of managers would then be compared. In all, four compositions of management pair were made and examined:

1. Senior manager and middle manager.
2. Middle manager and staff (i.e. a producer of control information for that middle manager).
3. Senior manager and staff.
4. Two staff, where two or more were supplying information to the same middle managers.

As the procedure employed in pairing the managers interviewed was a little complex, it is perhaps best illustrated by diagrams. Fig. 5.1 refers to the simplest case. In this, one staff only supplied the middle manager with significant volumes of information. Here, three management pairs were obtained:

1. The senior and the middle manager (AB).
2. The senior manager and the staff (AC).
3. The middle manager and the staff (BC).

A more complex case is shown in Fig. 5.2 with two staff

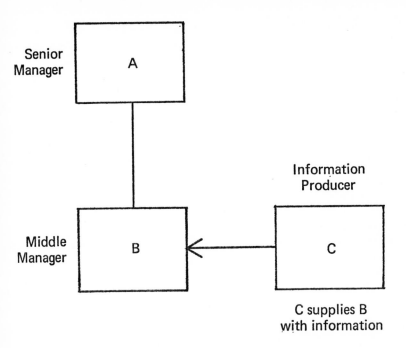

Management Pairs : Simple Case

Senior Manager — A

Information Producer

Middle Manager — B ← C

C supplies B with information

Three management pairs are obtained here:

AB   BC   AC

FIG. 5.1

supplying the middle manager. Doubling the number of information producers here doubles the number of pairs obtained, to six:

1. The senior and the middle manager (AB).
2. The senior manager and one staff (AC).
3. The middle manager and one staff (BC).
4. The senior manager and the second staff (AD).
5. The middle manager and the second staff (BD).
6. The two staff (CD).

More complex cases were compared on similar lines.

Management Pairs : More Complex Case

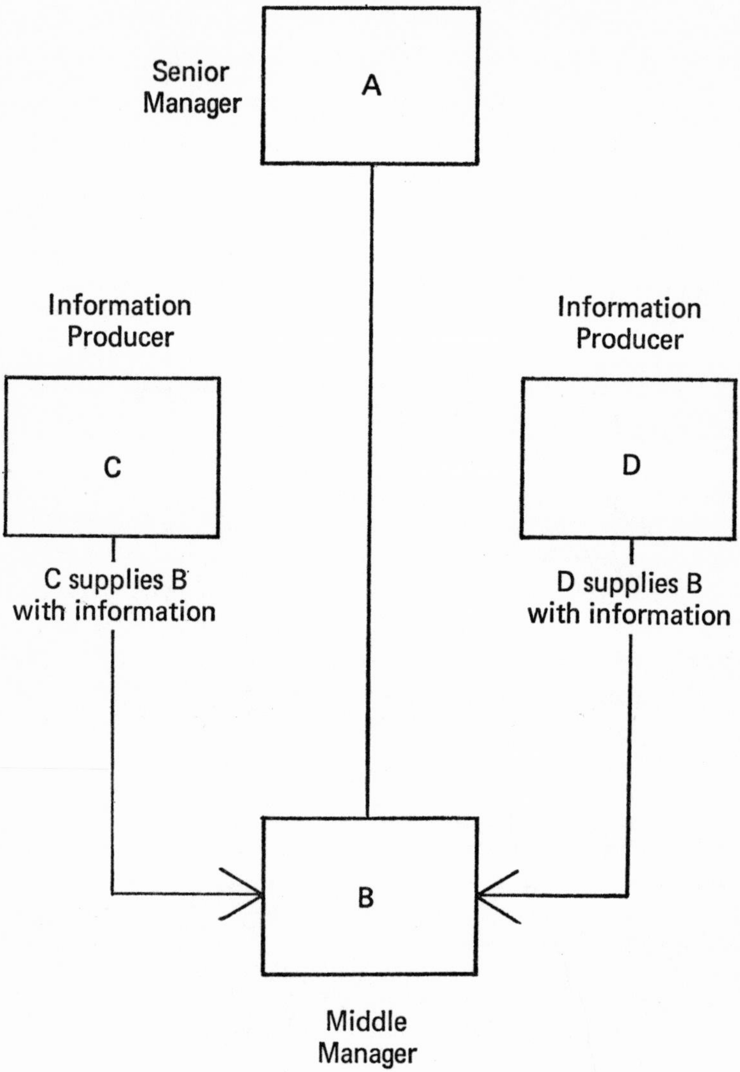

Senior Manager — A

Information Producer — C

Information Producer — D

C supplies B with information

D supplies B with information

B

Middle Manager

Six Management Pairs are obtained here

AB AC AD BC BD CD

Fig. 5.2

6 Differing Views of Middle Management Responsibilities

This chapter deals with four topics:

1. How to measure the degree of agreement between managers as to the identification of the success criteria appropriate for a particular middle management job.
2. The results obtained from applying this measure.
3. How to measure the degree of agreement as to the ranking of the success criteria for a particular middle management job.
4. The results obtained from applying this measure.

A remarkably low degree of agreement was found in all companies both as to the identification and the ranking of success criteria.

A. MEASURING AGREEMENT ON SUCCESS CRITERIA IDENTIFICATION

Senior managers, middle managers and the staff providing control information in five different companies having all identified what they thought to be the success criteria of specified middle management jobs, their replies had been arranged by management pairs.

The next step was to measure the degree of agreement between them and then to compare the degrees of agreement for the four compositions of management pair. The application of quantitative methods to ascertain degrees of personal agreement or disagreement on matters of opinion is not to be taken as producing results of the degree of precision to be found in the physical sciences. Nevertheless, it is a necessary and inevitable method of making comparisons, always bearing in mind the relatively unsatisfactory nature of the evidence and accepting that the results are indicative only and do not presume to have an unquestionable validity.

The most obvious way of assessing the degree of agreement between two managers might be to see how many criteria were identified by both managers. But such an approach may yield misleading results.[1]

Attention was therefore concentrated on proportions rather than on absolute numbers. For each pair of managers the number of success criteria identified by both was divided by the number identified by each, and the result expressed as a percentage.[2]

Manager A	Manager B
1. *Producing to production schedules*	1. *Meeting quality standards*
2. *Meeting quality standards*	2. *Producing to production schedules*
3. Cutting down material waste	3. Minimising unexpected down-time
4. Keeping straight-time labour costs within budget	4. *Minimising frequency and severity of accidents*
5. Controlling overtime	5. *Watching lateness, absenteeism and labour turnover*
6. *Watching lateness, absenteeism and labour turnover*	
7. *Minimising frequency and severity of accidents*	

Fig. 6.1

[1] This may be illustrated by an example. Consider two superior–subordinate management pairs, pair 1 and pair 2. Of the success criteria identified by pair 1 for the subordinate's job, let us suppose that only three are identified by both superior and subordinate. Suppose further that the managers in pair 2 identify five success criteria in common for the subordinate's job. On the face of it, the degree of agreement is greater between the managers in pair 2 than it is between the managers in pair 1. But if each of the managers in pair 1 identified only four success criteria, while each of the managers in pair 2 identified twelve criteria, pair 1 could be said to have the greater degree of agreement on the grounds that they had well over half their success criteria in common while pair 2 had less than half their success criteria in common. Hence the absolute number of success criteria identified in common may be a poor guide to the degree of agreement on success criteria between two managers.

[2] For example, in Fig. 6.1 senior manager A and his subordinate manager B are asked in separate interviews about the success criteria of manager B's job. Manager A identifies seven criteria. Manager B identifies five. Of the total of twelve, four (shown in italics) are identified by both manager A and manager B – eight, therefore, by one or the other. The proportion of success criteria in common is taken to be 4/8 or 50 per cent.

The results obtained

The data obtained on proportions of success criteria identified in common are shown in Table 6.1. For all four compositions of management pair together, the average proportion of success criteria held in common is 57 per cent.

Table 6.1

THE EXTENT TO WHICH PAIRS OF MANAGERS AGREED ON
THE SUCCESS CRITERIA OF SPECIFIED MIDDLE
MANAGEMENT JOBS

Composition of pair	Proportion of criteria held in common				
	0–20%	21–40%	41–60%	61–80%	81–100%
Senior manager and immediate subordinate	3	9	14	15	8
Middle manager and information producer	9	8	18	41	15
Senior manager and information producer	8	13	3	13	9
Two information producers	2	2	4	4	6
Total no. of pairs	22	32	39	73	38

Note: Average for all four compositions of management pair is 57 per cent.

This is indeed a low proportion, particularly when it is considered that the use of prompting cards may to some extent have influenced managers towards a higher degree of agreement than obtained in reality.

The question has been posed, whether differences of view between managers and functional staff concerning the success criteria of middle management jobs might perhaps account for the low degree of agreement already found between managers and staff as to the value of the information supplied to middle managers for control purposes. This question will have to be answered, but there was no doubt about the extent of the differences of view.

Analyses of variance

Did these differences reflect some failure by the staff information producers to understand the nature of the critical aspects of the middle management jobs, or a disagreement between the middle managers and their immediate line superiors?[1]

This question could be examined only by the application of an analysis of variance. If the differences were primarily between information producers and information recipients, then those management pairs in which one was an information producer would have, on average, a lower proportion of success criteria in common than either pairs composed of a senior and a middle (line) manager or pairs composed of two staff information producers.

The data for the analysis of variance are shown in Table 6.2.

Table 6.2

ARITHMETIC MEAN VALUES OF THE PROPORTION OF SUCCESS
CRITERIA IN COMMON (BY COMPANY AND COMPOSITION
OF PAIR)
(percentages)

Composition of pair	Company H	Company J	Company K	Company L	Company M
Senior manager and immediate subordinate	50	59	47	60	63
Middle manager and information producer	35	72	65	72	62
Senior manager and information producer	31	39	74	85	71
Two information producers	65	69	89	65	18

Note: It will be noted that the values of the proportion of success criteria in common vary both as between different companies and as between different compositions of management pair in such a way as to form a complex pattern of interaction.

In carrying out the analysis, two sources of variation had to be taken into account.[2] These were:

1. Variation as between different compositions of management pair.

[1] A further possibility might be that differences of opinion were associated with a particular managerial function. The 32 superior–subordinate pairs composed of production managers showed a higher average proportion of success criteria in common (59 per cent) than did the 17 superior–subordinate pairs concerned with sales (51 per cent). However, a two-tailed *t* test with 47 degrees of freedom gave a value for *t* of 1·18, which is not significant at the 5 per cent level.

[2] An additional complication was that the circumstances of the study

2. Variation as between management pairs with the same composition but in different companies.

The results obtained may be tabulated as follows:

Source of variation	Degrees of freedom	Sum of squares	Mean square	Value of F
Interaction	12	26,096	2175	
				3·54
Individual management pairs	184		614·4	

With these degrees of freedom, the value of F is significant at the 5 per cent level. Hence the hypothesis of significant interaction must be accepted. It is not therefore possible to say that the proportions of success criteria held in common varied significantly as between the different compositions of management pair.

The value of the proportion of success criteria in common for a given management pair was found to depend both on the composition of that management pair and on the company in which that management pair was located. With the data available, the effect of different compositions of management pair could not be separated from the effect of different companies.

It was not possible, therefore, to say whether larger differences of opinion lay between the information producers and the middle managers, or between the middle managers and their immediate superiors. However, some light is thrown on these differences when we consider the extent to which senior managers, middle managers and information producers agreed in their rankings of success criteria.

---

made it impossible to obtain the same number of management pairs in each category. For example, the number of superior–subordinate management pairs in company H differed from the number of superior–subordinate pairs in company J, and the number of superior–subordinate pairs in company H also differed from the number of subordinate–information producer pairs in company H. To deal with this problem of unequal cell frequencies, the method of fitted constants was employed. See G. W. Snedecor and W. G. Cochran, *Statistical Methods*, 6th ed. (Ames, Iowa: Iowa State U.P., 1967) pp. 488–93.

B. MEASURING AGREEMENT ON SUCCESS CRITERIA RANKING

Managers were asked to rank in order of importance the success criteria that they had identified as appropriate for a particular middle management job. The purpose was to measure the degree of agreement on ranking between the managers in a pair. Only those success criteria which were mentioned by both managers in a management pair were used in this ranking. This restriction was imposed in order to keep the question of ranking away from the problem of agreement on identification.

An example of the calculation is shown in Fig. 6.2. This covers the simplest case, in which both managers in a management pair identified the same number of success criteria.

A difficulty encountered in devising an appropriate measure of ranking agreement was that no restriction was placed on the number of success criteria that a manager could identify as appropriate to a particular job.[1] This made it necessary to have a measure which could deal with cases in which the two managers in a management pair each identified different numbers of success criteria.

This measure will be called the Index of Criterion Divergence (see below).

For those complex cases in which the managers identified different numbers of success criteria, reference may be made to Appendix C, in which the method of calculation is set out in detail.[2]

[1] The placing of such a restriction would have 'guided' managers' replies to an unacceptable extent. It would also have made it impossible to compare the numbers of success criteria identified by senior and by middle managers. This comparison showed there to be no significant association between the number of success criteria identified by a superior for a subordinate's job and the number of criteria identified by that subordinate for his own job ($r = 0.19$, $n = 49$). Taking the number of distinct success criteria identified for a job as a measure of the complexity of that job, it would thus seem that senior and middle managers did not agree closely as to the complexity of particular middle management jobs.

[2] The method outlined in Appendix C is related to that used in L. R. Hoffman, J. J. Hooven, N. R. F. Maier and W. H. Read, *Superior–Subordinate Communication in Management*, Research Study No. 52 (New York: American Management Association, 1961). That study, however, was concerned with a different aspect of management communication. It did not employ the

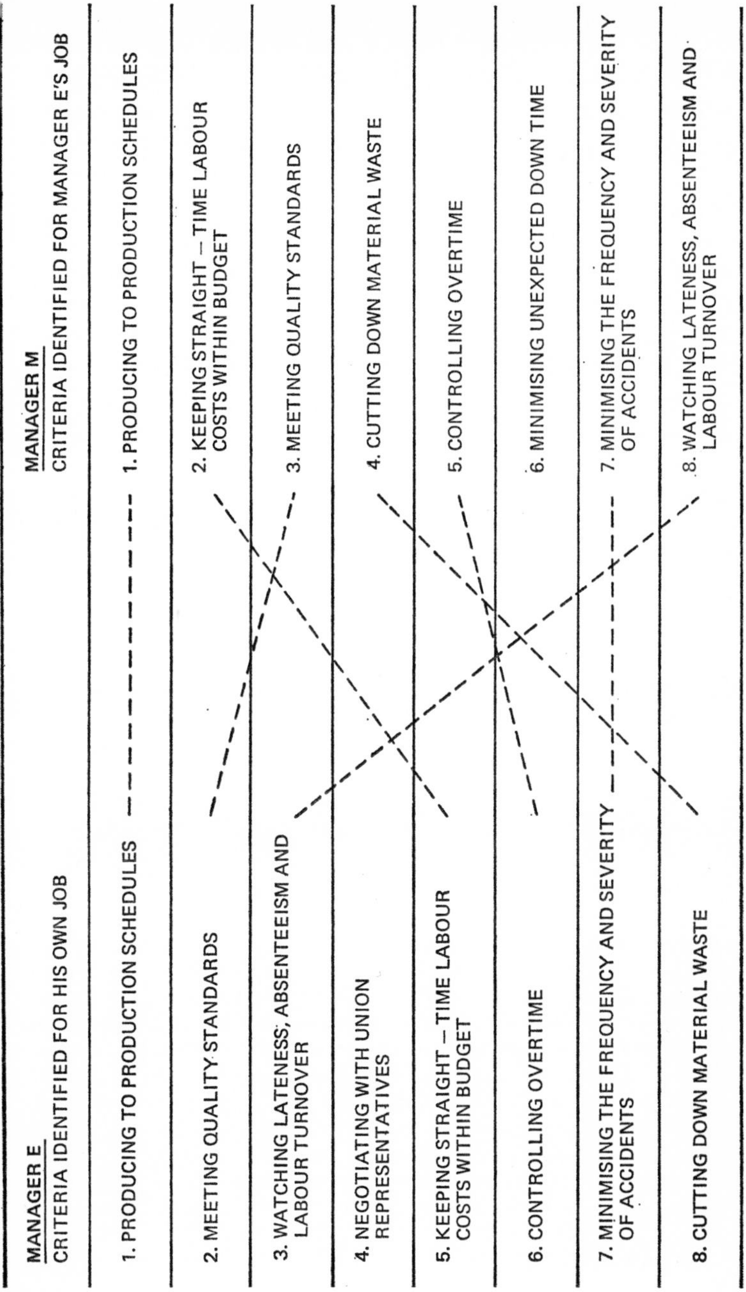

MANAGER E
CRITERIA IDENTIFIED FOR HIS OWN JOB

1. PRODUCING TO PRODUCTION SCHEDULES

2. MEETING QUALITY STANDARDS

3. WATCHING LATENESS, ABSENTEEISM AND LABOUR TURNOVER

4. NEGOTIATING WITH UNION REPRESENTATIVES

5. KEEPING STRAIGHT — TIME LABOUR COSTS WITHIN BUDGET

6. CONTROLLING OVERTIME

7. MINIMISING THE FREQUENCY AND SEVERITY OF ACCIDENTS

8. CUTTING DOWN MATERIAL WASTE

MANAGER M
CRITERIA IDENTIFIED FOR MANAGER E'S JOB

1. PRODUCING TO PRODUCTION SCHEDULES

2. KEEPING STRAIGHT — TIME LABOUR COSTS WITHIN BUDGET

3. MEETING QUALITY STANDARDS

4. CUTTING DOWN MATERIAL WASTE

5. CONTROLLING OVERTIME

6. MINIMISING UNEXPECTED DOWN TIME

7. MINIMISING THE FREQUENCY AND SEVERITY OF ACCIDENTS

8. WATCHING LATENESS, ABSENTEEISM AND LABOUR TURNOVER

FIG. 6.2

When the same number of success criteria were identified by both managers in a management pair, the calculation of the Index was as follows. First, the success criteria identified by each manager were arranged in the manager's order of priority. The lists of success criteria were then divided into segments corresponding to the number of criteria identified. This division is shown by the continuous lines in Fig. 6.2.[1]

The next step was to look for the criteria which appeared on both lists and to draw a broken line between the corresponding criteria. The number of units of difference was obtained by adding the number of continuous (segment) lines crossed by the broken lines. Thus for the management pair on the diagram there were 14 units of difference.

The more criteria are held in common, the greater is the maximum possible number of units of difference.[2]

What was required was a measure of the degree of agreement between two managers on the ranking of success criteria which was independent of the number of success criteria held in common. Thus it was not appropriate to use the number of units of difference as a measure of the degree of agreement. Instead, a measure was taken of the average number of units of difference in ranking per success criterion identified by both managers (the Index of Criterion Divergence), defined by the following formula:

$$\frac{\text{The number of units of difference in the ranking of success criteria by a management pair}}{\text{The number of success criteria identified by both managers in a management pair}}$$

Index of Criterion Divergence, which was devised to meet the special problems of this study. A number of other modifications were also made to the method employed in the above-mentioned work.

[1] The data on the diagram relate to a pair of managers interviewed in company M. This management pair were chosen for illustration because their Index of Criterion Divergence is particularly simple to calculate.

[2] This point may be illustrated by a simple example. Suppose two managers each identify three success criteria as being appropriate to a specified middle management job. If only one of these success criteria is identified by both managers, then their maximum number of units of difference is two. But if the managers agree perfectly on the identification of success criteria, both identifying the same three criteria, then their maximum number of units of difference is four.

For the example shown in Fig. 6.2, there are 7 pairs of success criteria. Since there are 14 units of difference, applying the formula above gives a value for the Index of Criterion Divergence of 2, that is, 14 ÷ 7. The meaning of this value is that for the management pair in the diagram there are on average 2 units of difference per success criterion identified by both managers.

It should be noted that the Index obtained is one of criterion *divergence*, so that as the extent of disagreement on ranking *increases*, the value of the Index *rises*.

If there were perfect agreement on the ranking of those success criteria which the two managers held in common, the Index of Criterion Divergence would have a value of zero. For management pairs in which the two managers had no success criteria in common, the Index of Criterion Divergence was not calculated. In such cases, if the Index were to be applied, a value of zero would also be obtained which would be entirely misleading, for it would suggest a perfect agreement on ranking rather than an absence of any agreement on the success criteria as such.

The values of the Index of Criterion Divergence obtained for the management pairs which had at least one success criterion in common are shown in Table 6.3. In this table, the arithmetic

Table 6.3

VALUES OF THE INDEX OF CRITERION DIVERGENCE

Composition of pair	Values of index			
	0–1·0	1·01–2·0	2·01–3·0	3·01–4·0
Senior manager and immediate subordinate	3	32	11	3
Middle manager and information producer	23	40	22	1
Senior manager and information producer	10	27	4	–
Two information producers	3	6	8	–
Total no. of pairs	39	105	45	4

Note: The arithmetic mean for all compositions of management pair together is 1.63.

mean value for the Index is 1·63. That is, for the four compositions of management pair taken together, there were found to be on average 1·63 units of difference in the rankings given by a pair of managers to a success criterion identified by both the managers in that pair. If there were perfect agreement on the ranking of success criteria, there would be no units of difference and consequently an average Index value of zero.

The question then arises whether these differences of opinion reflected primarily disagreements between middle managers and information producers, or disagreements between middle managers and their immediate superiors.[1] Inquiry into this question requires the use of a two-way analysis of variance employing the method of fitted constants, as before. The results of the analysis may be tabulated as follows:

Source of variation	Degrees of freedom	Sum of squares	Mean square	Value of F
Company	4	8·05	2·01	3·82
Composition of management pair	3	0·39	0·13	0·247
Interaction	12	1·22	0·102	0·193
Individual management pairs	173		0·527	

Examination of these results shows that the only source of variation which is significant at the 5 per cent level is the variation as between management pairs with the same composition but in different companies.[2] The way in which arithmetic mean values of the Index of Criterion Divergence were found to vary from company to company for each composition of management pair is illustrated in Table 6.4.

There was no significant difference in the Index values obtained as between different compositions of management pair.

[1] As with the identification of success criteria, there was found to be no significant difference between superior–subordinate pairs composed of production managers and superior–subordinate pairs concerned with sales. The average value of the Index of Criterion Divergence for the production managers was 1·59, and for the sales managers 1·58.

[2] It is outside the scope of this study to attempt to explain in detail why the degree of agreement on the ranking of middle management success criteria (as measured by the Index of Criterion Divergence) varied significantly from company to company. Results obtained from a small number of companies, as here, are in any case indicative rather than conclusive.

From Table 6.4 it is clear that even for success criteria identified by both managers in a management pair, which is only a small proportion of the total criteria they selected between them, there was typically substantial disagreement as to the appropriate ranking of these success criteria in order of importance.

Table 6.4

ARITHMETIC MEAN VALUES OF THE INDEX OF CRITERION DIVERGENCE (BY COMPANY AND COMPOSITION OF PAIR)

Composition of pair	Company H	Company J	Company K	Company L	Company M
Senior manager and immediate subordinate	1·6	1·1	1·7	1·9	1·5
Middle manager and information producer	1·1	1·5	1·7	1·6	1·9
Senior manager and information producer	1·1	1·5	1·6	1·4	1·7
Two information producers	0·9	1·4	1·9	1·5	2·1

Note: It will be noted that the values of the Index of Criterion Divergence varied considerably as between different companies, but relatively little as between different compositions of management pair within the same company.

But it was not a case of senior and middle managers being in close agreement, and facing a failure by the information producers to understand the nature of the middle management jobs. Nor was it a case of the information producers agreeing with the middle managers, but being opposed by the differing views of senior managers.

Differences of opinion in the ranking of the success criteria to be applied to the middle managers' jobs were widespread. They were not confined to any particular composition of pairs of managers. The information producers disagreed with senior and middle managers as much as senior and middle managers disagreed among themselves, and the information producers in turn disagreed among themselves.

Such wide divergences of view, both as to the identification and as to the ranking of the success criteria with which to judge middle managements' performance, necessarily imply the existence of considerable differences of view about the relative importance of what middle management does, or tries to do, or is believed to do. Such differences of emphasis have obvious and fundamental implications for the supply of management control information. For example, in the R group of studies it was found that, of 50 budgetary control returns which were followed up by higher management either in formal discussions or informal meetings, it appeared that 42 had been studied by the middle managers. Of 35 budgetary control returns which were not followed up in this way by higher management, no fewer than 30 appeared to have been disregarded by the middle managers. Thus follow-up by the senior management appeared to exert a powerful influence on the motivation of managers with regard to their control information.

This finding was further examined by the authors in the light of the results concerning success criteria. They covered all management control information, not budgetary control information alone as in the R studies.[1] As Table 6.5 shows, the extent of senior managements' follow-up was confirmed as a

Table 6.5

THE EXTENT TO WHICH MIDDLE MANAGERS CONCENTRATED
ON ITEMS OF CONTROL INFORMATION IN WHICH THEY
THOUGHT THAT THEIR IMMEDIATE SUPERIORS
APPEARED TO BE INTERESTED

	No. of items USED *by the middle managers*	*No. of items* NOT USED *by the middle managers*
No. of items in which the superior was believed by the middle manager to be interested	122	31
No. of items in which the superior was believed by the middle manager not to be interested	45	102

[1] In order to isolate as far as possible any relationship between use of information due to follow-up by senior management, and use for other reasons, only those items were considered which were used by some of the managers within a given company, and which were not used by other managers within that company. By considering the same item given to different managers, some of whom were followed up on it by the senior management, and some of whom were not, an attempt was made to approximate to the conditions of a controlled experiment in which all the other determinants of use except follow-up were held constant.

critical determinant[1] of the extent to which an item of control information was used by the middle managers, who were evidently most concerned with items relating to aspects of their performance about which senior managers asked questions and seemed to display an interest.[2] But nevertheless, they might or might not agree with their seniors that these *were* the most critical aspects. These studies suggest substantial disagreement.

[1] Analysis of Table 6.5 gives a value for chi-square of 66·4. This is an extremely large value, and with one degree of freedom is easily significant at the 5 per cent level.

[2] Further confirmation of this result is to be found in a recent American study by J. K. Simmons and M. J. Barrett, entitled 'A Behavioural and Technical Investigation into the Utilisation of Accounting Reports by Middle Managers'. This is to be found in T. J. Burns (ed.), *Behavioural Experiments in Accounting* (Columbus: College of Administrative Science, Ohio State University, 1972) pp. 351–414; see esp. p. 371.

7 How Differing Views
Affect Control Information

This chapter looks at some of the findings obtained concerning:

1. The overall evaluation of management control information.
2. The ranking of particular items of information for management control purposes.
3. The way in which agreement as to the identification and ranking of criteria for measuring the success of middle management in its job is related to agreement on the ranking of items of management control information.

The argument of this chapter is of necessity somewhat technical. Hence the reader whose interest lies mainly in the practical implications may wish to proceed directly to the section marked 'Implications' on p. 81. There it is shown that where managers disagreed as to the success criteria of a job, they usually also held differing opinions as to the control information relevant to that job. In these circumstances, any conclusion as to what control information should be provided was bound to be regarded as unsatisfactory from one point of view or another.

In the cases studied, the senior managers, middle managers and information producers all differed in their views as to the critical success aspects of particular middle management jobs. What consequences might such differing views have for the middle managements' control information? In pursuit of this question, managers were first asked to evaluate their control information and to rank particular items in order of importance. The relationship was then examined between these results and the findings obtained earlier concerning success criteria.

A. EVALUATION OF CONTROL INFORMATION

Each middle manager was asked to assign each item of control information he received into one of three categories:

1. Items considered to be vital, i.e. either a slight delay in their production or an inaccuracy in their content would be a matter of immediate personal concern.
2. Items considered to be of importance, i.e. frequent reference was made to them, although it could not be said that their production was vitally necessary for effective management.
3. Items considered to be either background or useless information, i.e. items which were thought to be substantially irrelevant to decision and action.

Similarly, the senior managers and then the staff control information producers in their turn were each asked to assign each item of the control information provided for a specified middle management job to one of these three categories, according to the value that was attached to that item of information for that job.

A comparison was then made between the proportions of items of control information assigned to each of these three categories of importance by senior managers, middle managers and information producers respectively.

This comparison is rather complex, and is best illustrated by an example.

Suppose that, in one of the companies examined, manager A is a senior sales manager, and reporting to manager A are three middle managers, managers B, C and D. Manager B is the Home Sales Manager (Northern), manager C is the Home Sales Manager (Southern) and manager D is the Export Sales Manager. Managers B and C are both home sales managers and consequently receive the same items of control information. But because manager D is concerned with exports, his control information differs from that of managers B and C. Manager A would see the cards[1] on which were written the items of control information provided to managers B, C and D, and would be

---

[1] These cards were similar in format to the prompting cards employed in the identification and ranking of success criteria.

asked to classify these items into vital, important but not vital, and background items.

To simplify this example, assume that managers B and C received only four items of control information, and that manager D received only three items. (In fact, managers in their position would normally receive a substantially larger number of items.) Suppose that the results obtained were as follows:

Items of control information received by managers B and C	*Manager A's opinion of the value of these items of control information to managers B and C*
Value of sales invoiced	Important but not vital
Value of orders received	Vital
Travelling expenses	Background information
Other selling costs	Background information

Items of control information received by manager D	*Manager A's opinion of the value of these items of control information to manager D*
Geographical analysis of invoices issued	Vital
Travelling expenses	Important but not vital
Other selling costs	Background information

These results would be summarised in the following way:

1. Manager A considered that there were two managers (B and C) for whom the value of orders received was vital.

   Manager A also considered that there was one manager (D) for whom the geographical analysis of invoices issued was a vital item of control information.

   Thus in all there were three occasions on which an item of control information was stated by senior manager A to be vital to a specified middle manager.

2. Similarly, manager A considered that there were two managers (B and C) for whom the value of sales invoiced was an important but not a vital item of control information.

   Manager A also considered that there was one manager (D) for whom expenditure on travel was an important but not a vital item of control information.

   Thus in all there were three occasions on which an item

of control information was stated by senior manager A to be important but not vital to a specified middle manager.

3. Finally, manager A considered that there were two managers (B and C) for whom expenditure on travel was an item of control information having little relevance, and three managers (B, C and D) for whom the amount of other selling costs was an item of control information having little relevance.

Thus in all there were five occasions on which an item of control information was stated by senior manager A to be of little relevance to a specified middle manager.

The above results would be tabulated as follows:

Category into which item of control information placed	*Number of times an item was described by a senior manager (in relation to the job of an immediate subordinate) as being in each category below*
Vital	3
Important but not vital	3
Background information	5

The same procedure would have been followed if manager A had been a staff information producer providing control information to managers B, C and D instead of the superior of those managers.[1] Further, in considering the opinions of middle managers B, C and D as to the value of their control information, the procedure would again be to add up the number of times an item of control information was stated by a manager to be vital, important or of little relevance to his own job.

The data obtained are shown in Table 7.1.

This table shows a contrast between the views of middle managers and those of their immediate superiors concerning the value of the control information provided to middle managers. The next step is to examine this contrast in more detail.

To carry out this examination, it is necessary to look at the relationship between the number of items of control information

---

[1] It should be noted that information producers were not asked to confine their evaluation and ranking of items of control information to those items which they personally produced. Each information producer evaluated all the items of control information provided for a specified middle management job.

identified by a senior manager as being vital to the job of a subordinate and the number of items identified by that subordinate as being vital to his job. If a senior manager considers that a large number of the items of control information provided to one of his subordinates should be vital to that subordinate, he is implying that this subordinate should in his job rely substantially on such formal control information. If the subordinate for his part considers that only a few of the items of control information which he receives are vital to him, there is clearly some divergence of opinion between superior and subordinate as to the value of control information provided for that subordinate's job.

Table 7.1

COMPARISON OF VALUES ASSIGNED TO ITEMS OF CONTROL
INFORMATION

	By a middle manager for his own job	By a senior manager for a subordinate's job	By an information producer for the job of a middle manager to whom he provides information
No. of items considered to be VITAL	153	214	455
No. of items considered to be IMPORTANT	173	165	330
No. of items considered to constitute BACKGROUND INFORMATION	157	137	289

Note: The application of a chi-square test to this table gives a value of 19·0. With four degrees of freedom, this is significant at the 5 per cent level. Thus there is a statistically significant difference in the proportion of items of control information assigned to the three categories of vital, important and background as between senior managers, middle managers and staff information producers.

In order to test whether such divergencies of opinion were commonplace among the managers examined, a study was made of the relationship between the number of items of control information identified as vital by senior managers and the number identified as vital by middle managers. This relationship is illustrated in Table 7.2.

It is clear that senior managers typically identified more items of control information as being vital for specified middle managers than those middle managers identified as being vital for themselves.[1]

Table 7.2

RELATIONSHIP BETWEEN NUMBER OF ITEMS OF INFORMATION
CONSIDERED BY SENIOR MANAGER TO BE VITAL TO
SUBORDINATE'S JOB AND NUMBER OF ITEMS CONSIDERED
TO BE VITAL BY SUBORDINATE

	Number of management pairs
Senior manager identified 7 more vital items than did subordinate	1
Senior manager identified 4 more vital items	3
Senior manager identified 3 more vital items	9
Senior manager identified 2 more vital items	3
Senior manager identified 1 more vital item	9
Senior and middle manager identified SAME NUMBER of vital items	10
Middle manager identified 1 more vital item than did superior	5
Middle manager identified 2 more vital items	8
Middle manager identified 4 more vital items	1
	49

Granted these differences in the overall evaluation of control information, the next question is how senior managers, middle managers and staff information producers differed when ranking items of information in order of the importance they should have for specified middle management jobs.

B. RANKING OF CONTROL INFORMATION

Each manager in a management pair was asked to rank in order of importance the items of control information provided for a particular middle management job. Since both the managers in a management pair ranked the same items, there was no need to use a complex method of comparing rankings. A simple measure of rank correlation was all that was needed.

The measure used was Kendall's tau coefficient, which was

---

[1] This proposition may be verified statistically by the application of a two-tailed t test for non-independent samples, with 48 degrees of freedom. The value of t obtained is $2 \cdot 44$, which is significant at the 5 per cent level.

preferred to the more usual Spearman's coefficient of rank correlation.[1] Having obtained the values of the tau coefficients, each coefficient was tested for significance.[2] A statistically significant agreement between two managers on the ranking of items of control information was defined to exist where the tau coefficient obtained from these rankings was significant at the 5 per cent level. The results obtained are summarised   in Table 7.3, which shows that only a minority of the management pairs agreed to a statistically significant extent in their rankings of the items of control information provided for a specified middle management job.

Table 7.3

AGREEMENT ON RANKING OF ITEMS OF CONTROL INFORMATION
PROVIDED TO MIDDLE MANAGER

Composition of pair	No. of pairs with SIGNIFICANT agreement	No. of pairs with NO SIGNIFICANT agreement	Total
Senior manager and immediate subordinate	22	27	49
Senior manager and information producer	12	34	46
Middle manager and information producer	19	72	91
Two information producers	4	14	18
Total	57	147	204

Note: A chi-square test may be carried out to establish whether or not the variation in the proportion of significant tau coefficients as between different compositions of management pair is significant. A value for chi-square of 9·60 is obtained, which with three degrees of freedom is significant at the 5 per cent level.

[1] This choice was made for two reasons. First, and most important, the number of items of control information ranked by a pair of managers was typically rather small. This favoured tau rather than Spearman's coefficient because the sampling distribution of tau converges rapidly to the normal form, while the sampling distribution of Spearman's coefficient converges rather slowly and has a number of peculiarities. Even for small values of n (n here being the number of items of information ranked), the distribution of tau, unlike Spearman's coefficient, is approximated relatively well by the normal distribution. The second advantage of Kendall's tau over Spearman's coefficient is that tau is easier to interpret.

[2] One-tailed rather than two-tailed tests were employed for this purpose.

Each manager might well stress those items of information which relate to the success criteria which he regards as most important. If managers are found to conflict in their rankings of success criteria for a job, it will not be surprising to find that these same managers also conflict when ranking in order of importance the items of information provided for that job.

The relationship between success criteria and control information may now be examined.

C. THE RELATIONSHIP BETWEEN SUCCESS CRITERIA AND CONTROL INFORMATION

In examining the relationship between success criteria and control information, it was necessary to ask two questions. These may be formulated as follows:

1. Did the management pairs who agreed in their rankings of items of information have a significantly higher proportion of success criteria in common than the management pairs who did not agree? (This question is examined in Table 7.4.)

Table 7.4

THE RELATIONSHIP BETWEEN THE PROPORTION OF SUCCESS CRITERIA IN COMMON FOR A GIVEN MANAGEMENT PAIR AND THE SIGNIFICANCE OF THE TAU COEFFICIENT FOR THE SAME MANAGEMENT PAIR

Composition of management pair	*No. of pairs examined*	*Value of point-biserial correlation coefficient*	*Significance of correlation coefficient*
Senior manager and immediate subordinate	49	0·699	SIGNIFICANT AT THE 5% LEVEL
Middle manager and information producer	91	0·380	SIGNIFICANT AT THE 5% LEVEL
Senior manager and information producer	46	0·374	SIGNIFICANT AT THE 5% LEVEL
Two information producers	18	0·217	NOT SIGNIFICANT AT THE 5% LEVEL

2. Did the management pairs who agreed in their rankings of items of information have a significantly lower Index of

Criterion Divergence than the management pairs who did not agree? (This question is examined in Table 7.5.)

The analysis of these two questions necessitated the use of an unusual statistical technique. While values were available for the proportion of success criteria in common and for the Index of

Table 7.5

THE RELATIONSHIP BETWEEN THE INDEX OF CRITERION
DIVERGENCE FOR A GIVEN MANAGEMENT PAIR AND THE
SIGNIFICANCE OF THE TAU COEFFICIENT FOR THE SAME
MANAGEMENT PAIR

Composition of management pair	No. of pairs examined	Value of point-biserial correlation coefficient	Significance of correlation coefficient
Senior manager and immediate subordinate	49	−0·413	SIGNIFICANT AT THE 5% LEVEL
Middle manager and information producer	86	−0·265	SIGNIFICANT AT THE 5% LEVEL
Senior manager and information producer	41	0·116	NOT SIGNIFICANT AT THE 5% LEVEL
Two information producers	17	−0·456	SIGNIFICANT AT THE 10% LEVEL BUT NOT AT THE 5% LEVEL

Criterion Divergence, the absolute value of the tau coefficient measuring agreement on information ranking could not be used in the analysis. The reason for this was that the value of a tau coefficient comparing control information rankings is affected by the number of items of control information ranked. Hence all that the tau coefficient could be used to provide was a statement as to whether or not there was a significant agreement between the rankings of items of control information made by two managers. Thus the data collected were continuous on one variable, but dichotomous on the other variable. For such data, the point-biserial correlation coefficient is appropriate. Point-biserial coefficients were therefore calculated to measure:

1. The degree of association between the proportion of success criteria in common and the significance of agreement on control information ranking (as measured by the tau coefficient).

2. The degree of association between the value of the Index of Criterion Divergence and the significance of agreement on control information ranking (as measured by the tau coefficient).

For the purpose of the point-biserial calculation, a tau coefficient which was significant at the 5 per cent level was assigned a score of 1, and a tau coefficient which was not significant at the 5 per cent level was assigned a score of 0. Taking a 5 per cent significance level for the purpose of testing the point-biserial coefficient, the results obtained were as shown in Tables 7.4 and 7.5.

These results may be summarised as follows:

1. Those management pairs who agreed as to which success criteria were appropriate for a given middle management job tended also to agree when ranking in order of importance the items of control information provided for that job.[1]

2. Those management pairs who agreed as to the order in which the success criteria for a given middle management job should be ranked tended also to agree in the order in which they ranked the items of control information provided for that job.[2]

IMPLICATIONS

The purpose of this section is to state in plain terms the implications to be drawn from the findings of this chapter.

To start with Table 7.1, this shows that the staff control information producers were significantly more satisfied concerning the value of the control information they provided

---

[1] In technical terms, there was (with one exception) a significantly positive association between the proportion of success criteria in common for a given management pair and the degree of agreement on the ranking of items of control information exhibited by the same management pair.

[2] This may be expressed in technical terms as follows. Apart from management pairs composed of a senior manager and an information producer, there was a significantly negative association between the value of the Index of Criterion Divergence for a given management pair and the degree of agreement on the ranking of items of control information exhibited by the same management pair.

for middle management jobs than were either the middle managers themselves or their immediate superiors. Dissatisfaction with control information would seem to come from information recipients rather than from information producers.[1]

In addition, Table 7.1 shows that middle managers were less satisfied about the value of the control information provided than were their immediate superiors. Table 7.2 confirms that the senior managers valued the control information provided to their subordinates more highly than did the subordinates who received that information.

Proceeding from evaluation to ranking, from the data of Table 7.3 it is found that a hypothesis of 'no agreement in ranking' must be accepted for over 70 per cent of the management pairs. This makes all too clear the magnitude of the disagreements between senior managers, middle managers and information producers as to the relative values of the items of control information provided.

Further study of Table 7.3 indicates significant variation in the extent of agreement as between different compositions of management pair. Superior–subordinate pairs showed the closest agreement, with the least agreement being shown by pairs composed of two information producers. The two compositions of management pair containing one information producer came somewhere in between.

When it is said that superior–subordinate pairs agreed most closely, it should be noted that even so under 45 per cent of these pairs agreed. Thus Table 7.3 hardly provides evidence of a close understanding between senior and middle managers as to the latter's information requirements.[2]

Finally, from Tables 7.4 and 7.5 it is clear that agreement as

---

[1] This tallies with a finding obtained from the first stage of the authors' study. In the majority of cases (41 out of 59) in which new items of control information were introduced, it was found that this was done primarily at the instigation of information recipients rather than information producers.

[2] Further evidence of a lack of understanding was provided by the fact that there were 19 superior–subordinate pairs in which senior and middle managers disagreed as to whether the latter's information was sufficiently comprehensive. In addition, of the 22 pairs in which the senior and middle manager both thought there was a gap in the middle manager's information, in only 6 of these pairs was there agreement as to what the gap was.

to the success criteria for a specified middle management job tended to be associated with agreement as to the ranking in order of importance of the items of control information provided for that job. This relationship between agreement as to success criteria and agreement as to the relative importance of the various items of control information provided, applied both to the identification and to the ranking of success criteria.

Where senior managers, middle managers and information producers disagreed as to the success criteria of particular middle management jobs, they generally took different views as to what control information was appropriate for those jobs. In these circumstances, the control information actually provided could not possibly cover all the success criteria considered by different managers to be important, and it was bound to be regarded as unsatisfactory from one point of view or another.

In Part III, attention is turned to the question of what can be done to improve control information.

Part III

This considers some of the implications of these research studies.

8 Information for Management Control

The following pages reflect some implications of these research studies in control information at middle management levels.

These reflections are largely in terms of ideas (shown diagrammatically in Fig. 8.1). There is no apology for this. The French accuse us as a nation of being weak in our grasp of ideas – though they allow that we are comparatively good at grasping facts.

It is to be hoped that at least some of the findings of these studies will speak for themselves. They suggest that in the field of management information (as indeed in a number of other management fields) there is a large and present need for more attention to what might be called 'first principles'.

Keynes, in a famous passage, concluded that we altogether underestimate the power of ideas. He added that by the time we have allowed them to influence us, the circumstances have often passed away, and they have probably ceased to have the slightest relevance to the problems of the moment.

If these ideas seem simple, all the better. Those who are interested in the academic jargon and the mathematics may refer to the five volumes of Ph.D. dissertations to be found in the library of Manchester University. But some simple ideas in management education will do us no harm.

REFLECTION I. TOP MANAGEMENT'S GRASP

Information for middle management is largely wasted, where there is no firm grasp of essentials by higher management.

Theories about the processes which are involved, or which ought to be involved, in decision-making are still fashionable in the literature of management. If the area of uncertainty is deep, if the number of possible alternatives is large, then the need for information will be great – i.e. all possible information which might throw light on the problem, or which might help to influence the results of a decision.

At the lower levels, where even management has a tendency to be repetitive, the assignment of probabilities is less important than at the higher levels of management. At higher levels, decisions are more non-recurrent – and it is therefore altogether more difficult, in practice, to assign probabilities based on previous experience.

Information may be classified on an operational data base. Pieces of information may be coded by reference to the alternative purposes to which they may be put. With the aid of a co-operative computer, appropriate information for each kind of decision can be produced quickly.

Information coding models may proliferate, with progenies of younger models, each appropriate for a different kind of decision. Each may include a wide range of alternative information. The prospects are exciting and apparently endless.

It may be possible in future to relate the costs of collecting information to its value. Until information has been collected, however, it is difficult to cost and its value is always to some extent a subjective judgement.

Those who tackle management information in cost–benefit terms have thrown a welcome light on this not uncommon problem of many managers. There seems to be masses of available information. It must cost a fortune to produce. Yet it never seems to be quite in the form in which the manager wants it, when he wants it, for the purposes with which he is having to deal.

But the assumption made by a number of theorists that management at the higher levels spends all its time carefully choosing between alternatives leaves something to be desired. In practice, management does not, generally speaking, work like that. It may hope to work in this way in some comparatively rare though important instances. But it is not the way that any management could conceivably run all of its organisation all of the time.

Management tends to be, in fact, a response. It is subject

REFLECTIONS ON A BASIC QUESTION:
WHAT DETERMINES THE EFFECTIVENESS OF
INFORMATION FOR MIDDLE MANAGEMENT CONTROL?

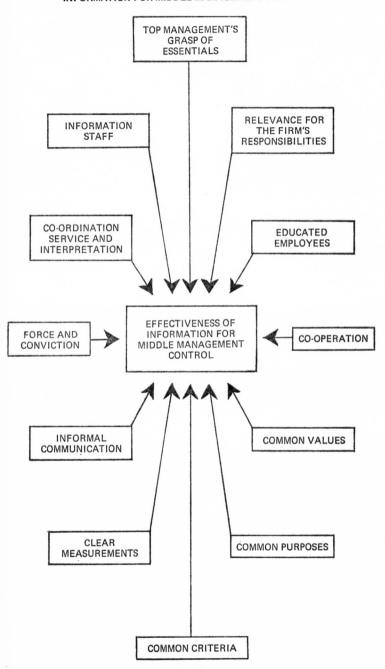

FIG. 8.1

to all sorts of pressures. It is open to all sorts of opportunities, both internal and external. It is often concerned to confirm or to recognise, perhaps in a formal way, what has already developed.

The reasons for managements' conclusions are likely to include deep-seated instincts. From these, political pressures are rarely wholly absent. Management may well be given information in order to substantiate what it has already, perhaps for other reasons, decided to do.

As decision-makers, managers tend to have very different personal temperaments. Equally successful managers take decisions in different ways. There are many different styles of management.

Some managers are not worried by uncertainty, prefer a high-risk policy, and rely on personal intuition. Others prefer low risk and a postponed decision approach.

Not only every kind of decision, but possibly every individual manager, may require a distinct and appropriate model.

This is in no sense to denigrate the need for more sophistication in the provision of information for middle levels of management. But first things must come first. In complex management situations, the challenge very often is to bring simplicity and order into the firm's affairs. The ability to identify main issues and to strip a confused situation down to its bare essentials is a talent which it may be extremely difficult in practice to acquire.

At the top management level, certainly in large and complicated industrial organisations, the successful management is not necessarily the one which is equipped with the most sophisticated apparatus and the most advanced management techniques. It is the one which succeeds in retaining a clear view and a firm grasp of fundamentals.

Without this ability in top management, the provision of more advanced information for middle management is misguided and a waste of resources.

REFLECTION 2. RELEVANCE

The relevance of control information for middle management depends on the extent to which it is seen to relate to the responsibilities, the purposes and the interests of higher management.

At the middle levels of management, management action is

even more of a response and even less of an independent process than it is at the higher levels.

Policy and direction may be matters for higher management. but control is essentially a middle management responsibility. The relevance of middle management's control information has therefore to be considered in a rather wider context than that of the manager's own department.

In particular, it has to be considered in the light of management's responsibilities – especially higher management's responsibilities.

At its widest, much misunderstanding between employers, employees, politicians and the public is due to a failure to clarify these issues of managerial responsibility.

It is no longer reasonable to expect an employee, even at the level of a managing director, to accept at its face value Dr Johnson's view that there is no pursuit more innocent than the pursuit of money; or Adam Smith's view that the material prosperity of society will be most rapidly advanced if the individual citizen is unhampered in his freedom to pursue gain.

But, at their widest, what are the responsibilities of higher management?

The industrial firm is more than an economic unit. Regardless of its political environment, it is the most significant social unit of our age. In Western so-called free society, it is commonly said that such a unit has manifold purposes, i.e. its management has to satisfy many interests, each having a stake in the firm.

Public ownership has proved to be largely irrelevant for the solution of problems for which private ownership had been held responsible. But the question of ownership continues to dominate much of the argument about managerial responsibility.

Rousseau once had a romantic image of a society of men equal in all respects. This has been widely translated as a call to return to an original Garden of Eden where all was held in common. It is thought that man, consequently, was then better behaved. The nasty economics of the private capitalist has upset it all – so turn him out!

Unfortunately, it now appears that the natural state of man, if given no discipline and nothing to believe in, is that of the juvenile delinquent. The original and the most primitive driving urge throughout nature turns out, after all, to be the possession of private territory.

The Russian peasant's colossal output of vegetables from his little private patch, which keeps Soviet Russia going, is a silent witness to human nature in the twentieth century.

The divorce of the professional manager from any real stake in the future worth of his firm is perilous for this worth. Ownership certainly affects motivation in a free society.

Whether he is the shareholder, or the state, or both, the owner of the business continues to get his full share of attention. This overshadows the image of the industrial manager's responsibilities.

The owner has much information about his estate, although he doesn't always believe this. Some other interested parties, bankers especially, may be able to state the information they want, and be in a position to require it. On occasion, the Stock Exchange may demand certain particulars. Under some Acts of Parliament, such as the Factory Acts, certain activities have to be disclosed to inspectors.

But does all this reflect the limits of reality in higher managements' responsibilities? What are his responsibilities, for example, in the eyes of the employees, including the middle managers?

To whom, and for what, is the firm (and for this purpose we may equate the firm with its higher management) exactly responsible? Are managers more than stewards for the shareholders? Do their responsibilities extend to the conservation of natural resources? Are they responsible not only to the shareholders, but also to the public as a whole?

Is management responsible in any measure either to, or for, its employees? Can management define this responsibility? Has it any responsibility to local society? If so, what is it?

Management control information has to be interpreted. It should be referable ultimately both to the interests and to the responsibilities of the firm. If these are not clear, then there is evidently not much point in paying too close attention to such information as is, or can be, made available.

In such a situation the problem, which may appear to be one of control and information, in fact lies elsewhere.

The ultimate questions of managerial responsibility are to be determined partly by law and partly by current national and international standards.

The law is all on the side of the shareholders. All one can say at present is that the law is unrepresentative of popular feeling. Managements' position is therefore anomalous.

Sooner or later, responsibility in respect of interests other than those of the shareholders must be defined. This may well be achieved directly by statute. Alternatively, Parliament may feel it to be more appropriate, as we are part of the Common Market, to define the powers and duties of a board superior to the executive board, composed of the representatives of various interests, and with powers to define *ad hoc* the responsibilities of the executive.

It was once so clear. The purpose of the firm was profit. Now it is so confusing. Management itself, when it looks into the future, is confused as to its purpose. But the managers of large companies in particular give more thought to this question, and are more concerned with the public interest, than is commonly credited.

Will the managers of multinational firms be held responsible to the government of the countries in which they operate? Will this responsibility include everything that they do worldwide?

Who is to say in future whether managements' responsibilities have been discharged?

By what standards is management to be judged? Is profit to be the only standard? Or will success politically, success in meeting national defence needs, or success in providing high-wage employment in advanced technological fields, have any relevance before a firm is to be declared bankrupt?

Who will decide these standards?

If the world will not continue to allow a vast discrepancy between real incomes per capita in different countries, will Western-based firms have to manage in future without the spur of growth? Will management have to succeed without profit? Or is this a contradiction in terms?

Will quite other criteria become fashionable or necessary, for example success in providing the public with a service? Can a public service be a service if it loses the public money?

Besides profit, service to the public has been advanced as the most important *raison d'être* of the industrial firm. But nobody has yet provided a satisfactory, generally agreed definition of what the term means.

It is not only the responsibilities, as such, which are under debate. It is also the question of how they are to be exercised. Perhaps one day we shall see the lessons of some centuries of experience in society at large applied to our industrial society in particular, with the separation of powers, the legislature laying down the rules, and a separate judiciary to see that the executive game is fairly played. The Industrial Relations Act, which is concerned with unfair practices and employee responsibilities, may even be seen as a small step in this direction.

It may be thought that we need a comparable Act for industrial managers, a new kind of Companies Act, specifically concerned with the responsibilities of industrial management. It would be no more popular, but may be just as necessary.

This is speculation, but it is the current speculation of thoughtful managers. If middle management is to exercise its best efforts for the firm, rather than for itself, then the responsibilities of the higher management to which it responds must be both clear and acceptable to middle management. This is not to be assumed.

REFLECTION 3. EDUCATED EMPLOYEES

Management education and management information are inseparable.

Information becomes valuable when its relevance is precise. The content of such information as it thinks appropriate to produce, its form and timing, are at present matters of management discretion. This discretion is not always well exercised.

For example, on the shop floor of most factories today the ignorance of the problems involved in the successful management of an industrial enterprise is quite extraordinary. Because they lack information, sensible and responsible employees are often in no position to combat the small but powerful minority of disaffected persons to be found in every factory. This minority seems to enjoy manipulating the majority in order to cripple the system on which the welfare of all evidently depends.

But if employees do not have adequate knowledge about the challenges, opportunities and difficulties facing the manage-

ment of the firm, who is to give it to them? The daily press? The
Church?

What is the responsibility of the management of the firm for
the education of its own people?

REFLECTION 4. CO-OPERATION

Co-operation depends on information.

Information about the firm for employees at all levels is
desirable, if not essential, because authority in industry has been
weakened.

The disciplines, the sanctions and the rewards of yesterday,
which made it possible for orders to be given with an assurance
that they would be obeyed, are pale shadows of their former
selves.

The very word 'obedience' has ceased to be an honourable
one. It is associated with underprivileged menials.

Wittingly or not, society has undermined the old authorities.
Management achieves results today, if at all, through some sort
of co-operation.

It is not impossible that co-operation may yet prove more
effective against competition than the disciplines which some of
our competitors still enjoy. If, however, we are to rely upon
co-operation, then we must recognise that co-operation is
dependent upon a sense of some common purpose. It involves
too a common sense of achievement.

Co-operation depends upon information, and employees at
every level now require information – truthful, up-to-date
information, in no sense restricted to their section of the enterprise. Such information also provides an indirect form of control.

REFLECTION 5. COMMON VALUES

A manager interprets his control information in the light of
what *he* understands to be an acceptable pattern of management
behaviour – the local conventions.

However, co-operation depends upon the acceptance of some
common values. And it is not at present wise or possible for
management to assume the existence of stable, commonly held
conventions (such conventions as might derive, for example,

from a shared educational experience, or from a shared pattern of religious beliefs).

Middle management is coming into power from a diversity of backgrounds. It reflects many differing and conflicting ideas – not least about the firm itself. There is a natural tendency for the present management to select men who apparently think and behave as the management does. But such men are hard to find.

It is rather more desirable at the present time, therefore, than might perhaps be the case under other circumstances, to make explicit the duties of the firm and of its managers at different levels, and the considerations which should be borne in mind when undertaking those duties.

For example, has the manager a personal duty to train his subordinate? If so, how does he propose to undertake it? Should he give orders, or explain the reasons for his orders, or explain the situation and avoid giving an order? Or is it all to be left to his imagination and to luck?

Many managers fail to go as high as they might, not from lack of ability, but owing to their manner or lack of it. What is expected of them is not fully understood. Their style of control therefore becomes inappropriate. Consequently, even when given relevant information, they may take irrelevant or harmful action.

REFLECTION 6. COMMON PURPOSES

Control information also loses its value if the purposes of higher management are doubtful. That it is all perfectly clear to the intelligent middle management is a large assumption often made by higher management.

There is something to be said in industry for the military concept that there must be one overriding, absolutely clear purpose; that everything and everybody is subordinate to that purpose; that all strategic and tactical objectives are set with a view only to furthering the attainment of that purpose.

Field-Marshal Slim stressed that, if those in charge of an operation take great pains to make quite clear what it is all about, and also that they will not be deterred by any obstacles, then the men involved can generally be relied upon to do what is required, with a high degree of assurance, and little reliance on orders.

If middle management is confused about the present purposes of higher management, it will not be helped by giving it more control information.

REFLECTION 7. COMMON CRITERIA

The value of the middle manager's control information is affected by the degree to which he finds himself in agreement with his superior as to what is to be regarded in him as successful or as unsuccessful management.

The particular aspects in which he is expected to show success must be quite clear to both of them. The critical element is the agreement.

How will his management be judged? If the middle manager knows this and agrees with it, he is then in a position to take decisions with confidence. Otherwise, what is the point of giving him more information?

He needs to know what is and what is not acceptable from him as a manager, at the particular level of management in which he finds himself.

He also needs to know the standards which will be applied to him – and what his attitudes are expected to be. These are just as important for him as, for example, his so-called terms of reference. This is his management style.

His role, his responsibilities, his resources, his cost budget, these can and should be defined. Equally important is a clear understanding of the terms in which his success as a manager will be measured. If management at any level is to support, and be known to support, the management at a lower level, there must be a specific agreement about managerial achievement.

Moreover, it is not sufficient for this purpose to bring down the tables from the mount. Each middle manager must have a very full and frequent opportunity to say what he is currently trying to achieve, to describe his difficulties, to say when he would appreciate help and in what way, and to ensure that his vision accords with the vision of his higher management.

Management must want to listen to the management which

responds to it. Managers often wish to catch the eye of the man above. They do not always want to listen to the manager below. In such cases, the management below feels a sharp sense of helplessness.

It may be thought that the managers are surely sufficiently clear, to the point that it must be perfectly obvious, on what is important and what will be regarded as good management. These studies confirm that managers need to challenge the nature of their own often sweeping assumptions as to what other managers see and what they think.

They suggest that the lack of agreement between managers as to what constitutes successful management is not infrequently more substantial than even a complacent management can well afford.

REFLECTION 8. CLEAR MEASUREMENTS

Control information for middle management should refer to performance in the essential features. What is essential must be agreed, and management must then agree how progress in each essential feature is to be measured.

To recognise the essential elements of successful management at a particular time calls for a considerable degree of management observation, attention and analysis. This is not something to be left to an accountant, or to any other functional specialist. It is a challenge to management to recognise the essential elements of their management.

Whether they are technological, or economic, or in the market-place, or in terms of human behaviour, these essential elements have to be watched. Any improvement or deterioration has to be observed.

If management is not to be left with a guess about this, there must be some applied measure. Some managers are good at guessing, and some are lucky. But management is a professional process.

Some essential interests are currently regarded as so intangible, and progress is said to be in such nebulous qualitative terms, that it is all best left to human judgement. Judgement is fallible. There is no more important task facing management in many companies than the introduction and development of a sound system of measuring progress in all its vital interests.

Lord Kelvin's dictum about numbers has been quoted too often to bear further repetition. But to measure progress in whatever constitutes successful management, and to avoid superficial conclusions, requires a system of relevant control measures.

As it is, it appears that the most advanced measures may be applied in some particular fields, while others confessedly quite as important seem to be almost entirely neglected.

This is not due to the total impossibility of introducing a measure. It is more probable that the attempt has never been made. What has been measured has been decided by the interests of those concerned with the technology of the measurements.

It may be difficult to measure precisely, say, the success of the management development programme. But management does much more difficult things than this every day.

It may be difficult to devise a measure for, say, the state of human relations. Yet if this is regarded as important, then it should not be beyond the wit of man to attempt, perhaps by a combination of labour statistics and periodical attitude surveys, to assess whether, for example, human relations in Factory No. 3 are currently improving or are going through the floor.

All sorts of relevant information about human relations is in the head of the personnel manager. Is it inconceivable that by quantifying this information a standard might be set? That deviations from this standard might be reported? That the reasons might be analysed? That progress in human relations, if this is a vital aspect of management, might be regarded as a normal everyday measure in the control information produced for the manager by those charged to measure such things?[1]

Are managerial attitudes important? Are employee attitudes important?

The middle manager cannot be expected to devote himself to the technical development of such measurements. However, he is entitled to state what he wants measured, and to agree the form and manner in which the measures are to be developed and

---

[1] Lord Justice Scrutton once remarked that the state of a man's mind was as much a fact as the state of his digestion. If important to management, they should both be determined.

defined by those made responsible for the management measurement system.

Formal written communication is no substitute for informal face-to-face communication: both are required.

Management control is primarily a middle management function. It has to be exercised in a human setting. It involves a human judgement. It is largely an exercise in social psychology.

The responsibilities of management, and the rules, and important decisions, should be reduced to writing. But there are strong arguments in favour of ensuring a well-organised system of verbal communication between managers, and an exclusive reliance on written formal control information at middle management levels will lead to disappointing results.

The informal system deserves at least as much care and attention as the formal. It is a mistake to imagine that this principle applies to smaller rather than to larger companies. Indeed, the contrary may be the case.

Face-to-face communication is, or should be, a two-way traffic. One of the first duties of any manager at any level ought to be to listen to what his subordinates want to say. Management communication in written form alone can be responsible for managerial stultification. Formality is needed in larger organisations. The danger is that it may become a substitute for intimate personal understanding.

There is some limit to the size of the firm that can be effectively managed without a considerable formality. Indeed, a case could be made for organising any firm into units none of which is too large for informal management. The maximum number of employees for this purpose is perhaps 500 or 600. Beyond this point it all becomes less clear to many employees, and more confusing to some middle managers. This has inevitable effects on managements' outlook. Indirectly, it affects co-operation and ultimately the economics of output. The so-called advantages of large-scale organisations are often hard to find in practice.

It is not to be conceived, therefore, that a good written

information system will be an adequate substitute for a well-organised system of personal communication.[1]

Many of the limitations, evident from these studies, on the value of the available formal information, would be overcome if the system of face-to-face discussion by managers at different levels of what they believe to be important matters were better organised.

These studies have been concerned only with written formal control information, at middle management level. Such information should form the basis for face-to-face meetings.

Identity of understanding between managers is further away than some managements appear to believe.

REFLECTION 10. FORCE AND CONVICTION

Whether middle management acts on its control information depends upon whether it is under pressure to do so.

The management machine turns only under the pressure of some force. In every industrial firm, there must be a driving force. In its absence the organisation will decline. Without it, individuals cease to care.

Force is not to be associated with an all-powerful dictator. Possibly every company needs a tiger, but there are other sorts of force.

Pressure from the top by men driven by a determination for achievement largely determines the effectiveness of the middle management. The great entrepreneurs created their own management teams. Middle managers respond to the outlook and behaviour of their superiors.

The force need not be self-advancement. It may be the influence of a message. Dedication and belief have notorious power over behaviour. Nor are the objects of dedication and belief confined to empire or religion. Much of industry was in fact developed under the influence of deeply held convictions.

---

[1] If, immediately after each management meeting, at higher levels for example, successive meetings are arranged for managers and employees in a descending scale, with an overlap of attendance, it is possible within a few days to ensure a very wide communication of important matters. This also provides a very ready and very necessary means of communication back again.

Obvious examples are the sanctity of capital, that to waste time was evil, that anything less than one's best effort was sinful.[1]

It is the responsibility of higher management to ensure this sense of force.

Some firms draw their life from a great idea – perhaps an old idea whose force is not yet spent, like the steam condenser, or a new one, like the mini-computer.

But youth is especially attracted to crusades, and to self-sacrifice for worthy causes. There are many kinds of crusade. Industry is in need of one. Social and economic conditions once offered high rewards for successful management and severe penalties for failure. To strive was economically essential. This may no longer be so, yet to strive for worthy objectives has no less appeal today than it ever had.

It is not enough for top management to have a purpose and to set an objective. Why should middle management want to achieve it?

The manager may be self-motivated from personal ambition or from inspiration. Or he may be under close scrutiny from on high. But middle management needs to feel a driving force. Otherwise it will settle down to a comfortable routine.

Management information is no substitute for management force.

REFLECTION 11. CO-ORDINATION AND
INTERPRETATION

Middle management requires an information service.

After playing with Leo, the early experimenters with this young computer concluded that it offered a superb opportunity not to centralise but to decentralise the management of the firm. Information could be centralised, but middle management in future must be able to decide the information it wanted and how to find it.

Not all firms in their computer developments have followed this path.

---

[1] Some may wonder today at Gladstone being so concerned as to go back in the evening to ensure that one of his private letters had not by chance been stamped with the official correspondence, because that would have been immoral.

Montgomery once remarked that you must never try to do it all yourself – or you will go mad. You must have a Chief of Staff. He added that the Chief of Staff would go mad – but you could always change him.

Some similar arrangement is needed for the industrial executive. He needs a staff officer for control and information.

The office of the Chief of Staff (Information) should not be concerned with the finer details of accounting, or costing, or production control, or technical development, or the construction programme. It should interpret and co-ordinate all important information on all essential aspects of the firm's progress.

The trends in all the features of the firm which management has decided are of vital importance should be watched together. The current position should be displayed in an operations room.

Managers cannot spend their time trying to interpret the meanings of all the information supplied to them, or available to them. However, the tide of formal written information in growing organisations cannot be ignored. The solution to some of it is, of course, just to stop it. But much of it is potentially important.

Its significance has to be considered, together with its implications for alternative courses of action. This is becoming a specialised task.

It is the task of a Staff Officer (Information) directly responsible to the management. Not a junior personal assistant, but a highly experienced and knowledgeable staff man, equivalent to a senior civil servant – possibly an executive transferred to staff information for a period as experience prior to further promotion.

Whether detailed planning should be included as a responsibility of the Chief of Staff (Information) is doubtful. He must display plans and he should be responsible for seeing that plans are made, and for comparisons of actual with planned progress. But planning is regarded by most managers with jealousy. They regard it substantially as their preserve. If they are not to plan their own management, then what are they there for?

Technical and economic forecasting and analysis is a specialist back-room activity, to enable top management to decide the broad strategies and policies, and to identify the opportunities and the constraints.

At each lower level, the management should be responsible, within such given policies and constraints, for thinking through its own plans and proposals. It should submit them for co-ordination with other plans and for ultimate synthesis.

This process can go very far. In some firms it goes down to the shop floor itself: operatives may be organised into groups and encouraged to offer advice to management.

Planning and operational control go together. Planning and management control go together. There are circumstances when the information officer may engage in detailed planning, but usually he had better not. He should be neutral. Planners are suspect.

The Chief of Staff (Information) should be responsible for the following:

1. Ensuring for each level of management that it is provided with the information service which it requires, i.e. ensuring that systems are installed to produce the information which the manager wants. This is not the same thing as centralising the service and then providing what it is thought the management wants or ought to want. It is not setting it up to suit the central executive manager, and then letting other managers have something whenever possible. It is the directly opposite philosophy of ensuring a local service of information by a member of the information staff, immediately next to and responsible to the executive manager himself – at whatever level.

2. Training the information staff who are to work with the managers (see below).

3. Ensuring that the information which the manager wants is provided in the language that he best understands.[1] The meaning that matters is the meaning for the manager who receives the information.

[1] The military services take trouble to ensure a common language: the terms are understood in the same sense by all ranks. General Morgan once remarked when planning 'Overlord' – the Allied invasion of France – that American and English generals, given identical memoranda, expressed in simple English words of not more than two syllables, were liable nevertheless to go off in opposite directions and do different things. Their interpretations were different. They attached to words and expressions subtly different meanings. This applies with even more force to the interpretation of figures.

4. Supplying an interpretation service. This involves:
    (*a*) confirming that the information given to the manager in fact conveys to him the meaning which the supplier intended it to convey, and that it is clearly understood;
    (*b*) considering with the manager the significance of the alternative courses of action which the information may suggest.
5. Going through with the manager a check-list of the assumptions which top management is making, and arranging for their validity to be examined periodically.
6. Interpreting the implications of the strategy and policy decisions of top management.
7. Receiving the first draft of managers' plans, in detail for the next year and in outline for a longer period.
8. Interpreting the significance of these plans for the benefit of top management. This involves analysis of the major features of the plans, not only in the obvious terms of cost and output but also in terms of their impact on labour relations and other aspects of management judged to be important.
9. Co-ordinating the plans as finally agreed, and checking that priorities are fully understood.
10. Identifying with the managers the vital elements in their plans on which success will depend and which will therefore require to be watched, and progress measured.
11. Proposing to management the measurement systems and the terms in which their own progress and the progress of their departments will be measured.
12. Developing new forms of measurement to ensure coverage for all features considered to be of importance.
13. Checking systems to ensure that the information supplied to the managers is satisfactory in terms of accuracy and speed.

REFLECTION 12. INFORMATION STAFF

It is instructive to consider the ideal personal characteristics of a Staff Officer (Information) and hence to consider his training, education and experience for the job:

1. He should have a quick grasp of essentials, and be able to

isolate from a mass of confused data the nature of the problem to be solved.

2. He should also have the intelligence, or the experience, and preferably both, to understand many 'languages', e.g. the languages of designers and of finance men, and of salesmen, and of estimators, and of general managers. All managers have contributions to make. Their points of view must be considered together.

3. He should be persuasive. The ability to persuade is much underestimated today. Rhetoric is no longer one of the cornerstones of education. Yet the power to persuade is important.

4. He must carry general confidence that he knows how to behave. For example, he should never pass comments on managerial performance, actual or proposed, to higher management, which he has not already discussed with the manager himself.

5. As he is there in order to provide a service to the executive line manager, he must avoid ever issuing instructions in his own name.

6. If he is in a large organisation, and appointed to be whole-time or part-time at the service of management down the line, he should first work in the information centre, understand what systems are being developed, and what they can currently offer.

7. He should be numerate, and enjoy instructing managers in the implications of the hieroglyphics which he employs.

8. He should be perfectly familiar with higher management's outlook, values and policies.

Conclusions

If the manager at the middle level is to exercise an effective control, he needs an exchange of information with the higher management to which he is responsible, in the following circumstances:

From the Top down to the Manager

A. *Concerning the Firm*

1. A clear understanding of the firm's opportunities, purposes and constraints. In particular, the overriding central purpose of the firm – what the firm is trying to do and how it is trying to do it.
2. A strong sense of direction and of commitment in top management.
3. A definition of what would be regarded as successful management of the firm.
4. An appreciation of how far the firm is succeeding or failing.
5. The opportunity to comment on this; in some organisations, even the shop floor is now wanting representation in policy decisions.

B. *Concerning his Department*

1. The policies, strategies and constraints which are given for him as a manager and within which he has to manage.
2. The central purpose of his own department, and how this relates to other departments' purposes.
3. The limits to his authority – hopefully so designed that he has all possible authority subject to stated exceptions, rather than a circumscribed and described authority.
4. What is expected of him – what matters most in his management.

5. How his management will be judged – the meaning of success or failure for him.
6. The rules of the game – what is and is not acceptable in his manner of management.

C. *The Interpretation of his Results*

1. Periodic confirmation of the above, with a statement of any shifts in emphasis or priority.
2. The immediate challenges to him as a manager.
3. What is wanted from him, with clear priorities.
4. The measurements, clearly distinguished, which will be used:
   (*a*) in assessing his department's progress;
   (*b*) in judging his success as a manager, over a limited period of time.

From the Manager to the Top

D. *His Response*

1. The manager's own appreciation:
   (*a*) of what is wanted of him and his capacity to achieve it;
   (*b*) of the additional resources which he considers he requires for different levels of achievement by him, by comparison with the resources which he now has;
   (*c*) of his constraints, and his proposals for dealing with them;
   (*d*) of what are the vital matters on which his own successful management and his department's success are considered to depend;
   (*e*) of the assumptions underlying his decisions;
   (*f*) of the validity of the measurements which will be applied in arriving at judgements as to the adequacy of his performance.

E. *Further Basic Requirements*

1. Agreement on objectives and priorities between the manager and those to whom he responds. It is the agreement, or the recognition of lack of agreement, which is all-important.
2. The quantification of the above. In so far as precise numbers are secondary to agreement in principle,

quantification can follow rather than precede agreement.

3. A routine programme throughout the year to ensure that each recognisable stage in the information process is part of a running timetable.

F. *An Information Service*

In small, intimate organisations much of the above may come informally – although the dangers of assuming managerial knowledge and understanding are generally underestimated even in the smallest firms. In larger organisations it is necessary to have more formal procedures, and to have someone in charge of the information process.

The role of a staff information adviser to executive management is partly filled in many British firms by a management accountant. In the United States, such an adviser may be called a controller. But the range of functions even of a relatively sophisticated United States controller would be much narrower than that described here for a Chief of Staff (Information).

The concept of a Chief of Staff (Information) is at the same time wider in its scope and more constrained in its authority than is the controllership concept. It maintains intact the staff/line distinction, which if blurred can lead to an over-centralisation of authority, thereby frustrating the need of middle management for decentralised independent decision-making in an increasingly complex and democratic business environment, within a clearly established set of economic and social responsibilities.

Managers Interviewed in the First Stage of the Authors' Study

In all, 129 interviews with managers were carried out in the first stage of the authors' study. The table below is a classification of the managers interviewed according to their function.

Function of managers	No. interviewed
STAFF MANAGERS	
Stock control information producers	5
Electronic data-processing managers	1
Management accountants	10
Financial accountants	7
Work study officers	2
Production planners	5
Officers responsible for personnel information	8
Training officers	6
Quality control managers	3
Research administration officers	7
Sales administration officers	5
Marketing managers	1
Public relations managers	5
	65
LINE MANAGERS	
Production managers	34
Sales managers	17
Research managers	5
Personnel managers	5
Stock control managers	3
	64

Managers Interviewed in the Second Stage of the Authors' Study

In all, 150 interviews with managers were carried out in the second stage of the authors' study. The table is a classification

Function of managers	No. interviewed once	No. interviewed twice
STAFF MANAGERS		
Stock control information producers	6	–
Electronic data-processing managers	1	1
Management accountants	2	5
Financial accountants	1	1
Credit control officers	1	–
Work study officers	–	3
Production planners	2	–
Officers responsible for personnel information	4	2
Training officers	4	–
Safety officers	1	–
Quality control managers	4	1
Production development managers	3	–
Sales service managers	3	–
Sales administration managers	–	6
Marketing managers	–	2
Public relations managers	1	–
	33	21
LINE MANAGERS		
Senior production managers	16	
Senior sales managers	10	
Middle production managers	32	
Middle sales managers	17	
	75	

of the managers interviewed according to their function. The managers who were interviewed twice were staff managers who on investigation were found to provide line managers with substantial volumes of written control information on a regular basis. By comparing for each staff management function the number of managers interviewed twice against the number interviewed only once, an assessment may be made of the extent to which each staff management function provided control information to line managers.

Calculation of the Index of Criterion Divergence for More Complex Cases

As was pointed out in Chapter 6, no restriction was placed in the authors' study on the number of success criteria that a manager could identify as being appropriate to a particular middle management job. There therefore arose a number of cases in which the managers in a management pair identified different numbers of success criteria as being appropriate to a particular job.

From the point of view of calculating the Index, the simplest of these cases would have arisen where the numbers of success criteria identified by two managers had a common divisor. In such a case, the two managers' lists of success criteria would have been divided into equivalent segments, the shorter of the lists determining the number of these segments. However, no case of this type arose. Where division into equivalent segments was not possible, the first 'extra' success criterion appeared in the last segment, the second 'extra' criterion in the next-to-last segment, and so on. The effect of this procedure was to reduce the extent to which managers were shown to differ in their rankings.

Two examples are given of this procedure. Fig. C.1 illustrates a case in which one manager identified seven criteria, while the other identified only six. This example is based on data from company M.

Fig. C.2 illustrates a case in which the difference was not one but two criteria, with one of the managers identifying eight criteria while the other identified six. This example is taken from company J.

The procedure illustrated in Figs. C.1 and C.2 was used for

all cases in which one manager identified more criteria than the other. In a few cases, however, an extension of this procedure was necessary. These were the cases in which one manager identified more than twice as many criteria as the other. In these cases, the bottom segment contained three of the success criteria of one manager together with one of the criteria of the other manager.[1] Segments above the bottom one contained two of the success criteria of one manager together with one of the criteria of the other manager. Again, this procedure had the effect of reducing the extent to which managers were shown to differ in their rankings. Fig. C.3, based on data from company L, illustrates this procedure.

MANAGER C *Criteria identified for his own job*		MANAGER L *Criteria identified for manager C's job*
1. Producing to production schedules	SEGMENT 1	1. Watching lateness, absenteeism and labour turnover
2. Meeting quality standards	SEGMENT 2	2. Producing to production schedules
3. Cutting down material waste	SEGMENT 3	3. Meeting quality standards
4. Keeping straight-time labour costs within budget	SEGMENT 4	4. Minimising unexpected down-time
5. Controlling overtime	SEGMENT 5	5. Minimising the frequency and severity of accidents
6. Watching lateness, absenteeism and labour turnover 7. Minimising the frequency and severity of accidents	SEGMENT 6	6. Controlling overtime

FIG. C.1

ONE MANAGER IDENTIFYING ONE MORE SUCCESS CRITERION THAN THE OTHER

This, then, was the procedure adopted for division into segments. The next step was to use these segments to provide

[1] In no case was it necessary for any segment above the bottom one to contain three of the success criteria identified by one manager together with one of the success criteria identified by the other manager.

a measure of the extent of agreement between two managers. In order to do this, it was necessary to identify the success criteria which appeared on both managers' lists and to draw a (broken) line between the corresponding criteria. Thus, in the example shown in Fig. C.4,[1] manager O's first-ranked criterion and manager Q's second-ranked criterion were identical and

MANAGER H *Criteria identified for manager K's job*		MANAGER K *Criteria identified for his own job*
1. Obtaining accurate sales forecasts	SEGMENT 1	1. Maintaining good personal contacts with important customers
2. Achieving the budgeted volume of sales	SEGMENT 2	2. Developing markets for new products
3. Developing new customers for existing products	SEGMENT 3	3. Developing new customers for existing products
4. Increasing the efficiency of representatives	SEGMENT 4	4. Carrying out co-ordination with production managers
5. Predicting competitors' activities 6. Maintaining sales margins at budgeted level	SEGMENT 5	5. Achieving the budgeted volume of sales
7. Obtaining favourable public relations 8. Keeping selling costs within budget	SEGMENT 6	6. Predicting competitors' activities

FIG. C.2

ONE MANAGER IDENTIFYING TWO MORE SUCCESS
CRITERIA THAN THE OTHER

were therefore connected by a broken line. Similarly, broken lines connected manager O's second-ranked criterion with manager Q's third-ranked criterion, manager O's third-ranked criterion with manager Q's fourth-ranked criterion, and manager O's sixth-ranked criterion with manager Q's fifth-ranked criterion. The other criteria were not held in common by both managers and were therefore not connected.

[1] The data on this figure are taken from company M.

Having done this, the figure representing the amount of difference in ranking (that is, the number of units of difference) was obtained by adding up the number of solid (segment) lines crossed by the broken lines. It should be noted that, in Fig. C.4,

MANAGER A *Criteria identified for manager B's job*		MANAGER B *Criteria identified for his own job*
1. Meeting quality standards	SEGMENT 1	1. Assessing the feasibility of proposed new production processes 2. Producing to production schedules
2. Producing to production schedules	SEGMENT 2	3. Meeting quality standards 4. Carrying out accurate forecasting to relate production activity to expected sales
3. Keeping labour costs within budget	SEGMENT 3	5. Cutting down on material waste 6. Checking that machine maintenance is properly carried out
4. Watching lateness, absenteeism and labour turnover	SEGMENT 4	7. Minimising the frequency and severity of accidents 8. Minimising unexpected down-time
5. Supervising mill labour training and promotion	SEGMENT 5	9. Keeping labour costs within budget 10. Watching lateness, absenteeism and labour turnover 11. Supervising mill labour training and promotion

FIG. C.3
ONE MANAGER IDENTIFYING MORE THAN TWICE AS MANY
SUCCESS CRITERIA AS THE OTHER

the success criterion ranked fifth by manager O and sixth by manager Q did not give rise to a unit of difference although the rankings were different, because no segment line was crossed. This again illustrates the tendency of this method of calculation

Fig. C.4. Illustration of method of calculating the number of units of difference

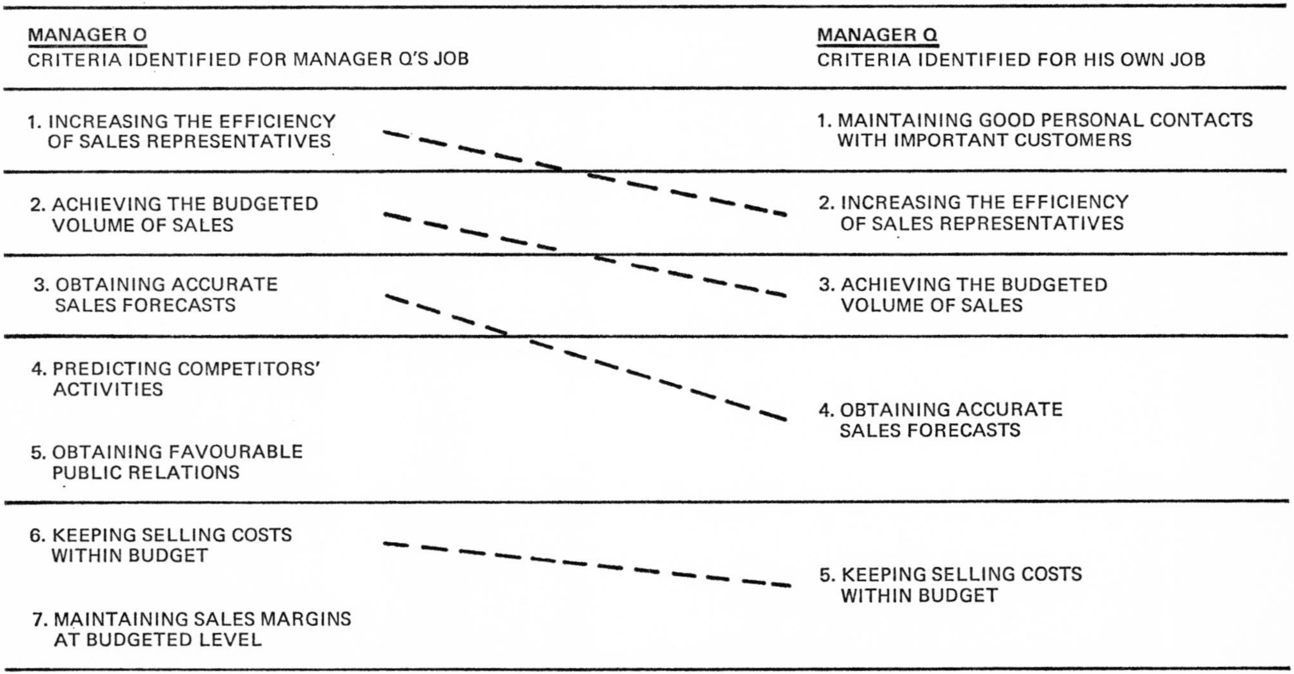

MANAGER O
CRITERIA IDENTIFIED FOR MANAGER Q'S JOB

1. INCREASING THE EFFICIENCY OF SALES REPRESENTATIVES

2. ACHIEVING THE BUDGETED VOLUME OF SALES

3. OBTAINING ACCURATE SALES FORECASTS

4. PREDICTING COMPETITORS' ACTIVITIES

5. OBTAINING FAVOURABLE PUBLIC RELATIONS

6. KEEPING SELLING COSTS WITHIN BUDGET

7. MAINTAINING SALES MARGINS AT BUDGETED LEVEL

MANAGER Q
CRITERIA IDENTIFIED FOR HIS OWN JOB

1. MAINTAINING GOOD PERSONAL CONTACTS WITH IMPORTANT CUSTOMERS

2. INCREASING THE EFFICIENCY OF SALES REPRESENTATIVES

3. ACHIEVING THE BUDGETED VOLUME OF SALES

4. OBTAINING ACCURATE SALES FORECASTS

5. KEEPING SELLING COSTS WITHIN BUDGET

to understate the extent to which managers differed in their rankings.

The example in Fig. C.4 shows three units of difference because the broken lines cross three solid (segment) lines in all. There are four pairs of success criteria (indicated by the four broken lines). The calculation of the Index of Criterion Divergence involves dividing the number of units of difference by the number of pairs of criteria. Applying this formula here, the Index of Criterion Divergence is given by 3/4 or 0·75. (That is, on average there are 0·75 units of difference in ranking per success criterion identified by both managers O and Q in Fig. C.4.)

Bibliography

Ansoff, H. I., *Corporate Strategy* (New York: McGraw-Hill, 1965).

Burns, T., and Stalker, G. M., *The Management of Innovation* (London: Tavistock Press, 1961).

Cochran, W. G., and Snedecor, G. W., *Statistical Methods*, 6th ed. (Ames, Iowa: Iowa State U.P., 1967).

Deming, R. H., *Characteristics of an Effective Management Control System in an Industrial Organisation* (Cambridge, Mass.: Harvard U.P., 1968).

Dent, J. K., 'Organisational Correlates of the Goals of Business Management', *Personnel Psychology*, vol. xii, no. 3 (1959).

Downs, A., and Monsen, R. J., 'A Theory of Large Managerial Firms', *Journal of Political Economy*, vol. lxxiii, no. 3 (June 1965).

Drucker, P. F., *The Practice of Management* (New York: Harper & Bros., 1954).

Emery, J. C., *Organizational Planning and Control Systems: Theory and Technology* (New York: Collier–Macmillan, 1969).

Evans, G. H., *Managerial Job Descriptions in Manufacturing*, Research Study No. 65 (New York: American Management Association, 1964).

Financial Executives Research Foundation, *Management Planning and Control: The H. J. Heinz Approach* (New York, 1957).

Hekimian, J. S., *Management Control in Life Insurance Branch Offices* (Cambridge, Mass.: Harvard U.P., 1965).

Helfert, E. A., May, E. G., and McNair, M. P., *Controllership in Department Stores* (Cambridge, Mass.: Harvard U.P., 1965).

Hoffman, L. R., Hooven, J. J., Maier, N. R. F., and Read, W. H., *Superior–Subordinate Communication in Management*, Research Study No. 52 (New York: American Management Association, 1961).

Hofstede, G. H., *The Game of Budget Control* (London: Tavistock Press, 1968).

Juran, J. M., and Louden, J. K., *The Corporate Director* (New York: American Management Association, 1966).

Lewis, R. W., 'Measuring, Reporting and Appraising Results of Operations with Reference to Goals, Plans and Budgets', contained in *Planning, Managing and Measuring the Business* (New York: Controllership Foundation, 1955).

Miller, E. C., *Objectives and Standards: An Approach to Planning and Control*, Research Study No. 74 (New York: American Management Association, 1966).

——, *Objectives and Standards of Performance in Marketing Management*, Research Study No. 85 (New York: American Management Association, 1967).

——, *Objectives and Standards of Performance in Production Management*, Research Study No. 84 (New York: American Management Association, 1967).

Moore, F. G., *Management* (New York: Harper & Row, 1964).

Sperling, JoAnn, *Job Descriptions in Marketing Management* (New York: American Marketing Association, 1969).

Stokes, P. M., *A Total Systems Approach to Management Control* (New York: American Management Association, 1968).